POSITIVE

PARENTING

Bringing Up
Responsible, Well-Behaved
& Happy Children

Revised and Updated Edition of
Bringing Up Responsible Children,
first published in 1999

John Sharry

VERITAS

First published 1999
This edition, 2008, published by Veritas Publications
7–8 Lower Abbey Street
Dublin 1
Ireland
Email publications@veritas.ie
Website www.veritas.ie

10 9 8 7 6

ISBN 978 184730 077 5

A catalogue record for this book is available from the British Library.

Copyright © John Sharry, 2008
Reward Chart images © Grainne Hampson, 2008
Cover image © Iva Villey, 2008

Printed in Ireland by W&G Baird Ltd, Antrim

Veritas books are printed on paper made from the wood pulp of managed forests.
For every tree felled, at least one tree is planted, thereby renewing natural resources.

Contents

To Grainne,
The Greatest Parent I Know

Introduction
Loving and Responsible Parenting

Getting The Balance Right

Positive Parenting · Positive Discipline

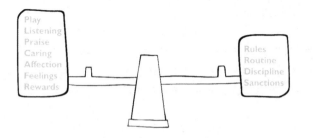

It can be hard being a parent these days. Parents are busier than ever and many of the traditional supports that we relied upon are no longer there. There is increased pressure on parents to 'get it right'. There are pressures to be positive and encouraging, while also being good disciplinarians, teaching our children right from wrong. We are also expected to be there for our children, supportively involved in their lives, while also holding down employment and providing for our families.

Good parenting is essentially about achieving balance. The key is to achieve balance between the needs of our children and our own needs as parents; between the need to encourage and love children and the need to provide them with rules and discipline.

In this book we argue that effective parenting involves achieving balance between Positive Parenting – providing your children with positive attention (through play/special time, listening, praise and encouragement etc.) – and also Positive Discipline – teaching children how to be responsible by setting clear rules and being firm about them. Both are essential in bringing up children well, teaching them how to behave responsibly and helping them be happy and emotionally secure adults.

Sometimes the problems in society are blamed on children not being cared for properly or suffering neglect as children (e.g. not experiencing positive parenting). Other times these problems are blamed on a lack of discipline in the child's upbringing – parents letting their children get out of control or failing to set proper rules. The truth lies somewhere in the middle: children need both loving and caring parenting as well as clear discipline and rules. The secret is getting the balance right.

Problems occur when the balance is out of kilter; when children do not receive enough encouragement, support and understanding and when they do not receive firm, authoritative parenting. This book is all about helping parents get that balance right.

Empowering Parenting

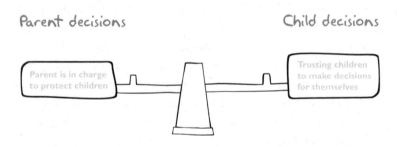

Parenting is also a balance between supporting children in making decisions for themselves and making decisions for them as parents; between allowing them to learn for themselves and protecting and teaching them. This is a challenging balance you have to get right as children grow up and one that you have to constantly renegotiate as they become increasingly independent. It is important as a parent to remember the long-term goal – to empower children to grow up into secure, happy adults who can make responsible decisions for themselves.

Many writers describe family life as like embarking on a plane journey together: you start the journey with a destination in mind and a navigation plan, but throughout the journey you can get thrown off course by other factors, such as wind or rain or other air traffic. Being off-course is in fact quite normal. As Stephen Covey, author of *The Seven Habits of Highly Effective Families*, says: 'Good families – even great families – are off track 90 per cent of the time!' What matters most is that you keep returning to your original course and you keep the destination in mind. Don't let events throw you off-course permanently – keep returning to the flight plan.

The metaphor of a plane journey also describes the long-term aim of parenting. When a child is born, the parent is in the pilot's seat, very much in charge of the controls. Parents make all the decisions about infants and young children's lives, about what they wear and where they go etc. As a child begins to get older, a good parent allows the child into the cockpit and begins to teach them how to operate the controls. The child begins to make some decisions for themselves and learns how to do some flying under the supervision of the parent. As the child becomes a teenager, they begin to fly their own plane, with the parent still present as a teacher/supporter, before proceeding to fly their plane as an adult.

Start With Caring For Yourself As A Parent

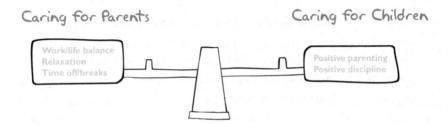

Caring for Parents

Work/life balance
Relaxation
Time off/breaks

Caring for Children

Positive parenting
Positive discipline

As well as caring for their children, it is also important for parents to prioritise their own welfare and personal development. This is another crucial balance that is important to achieve. Unfortunately, it is easy to get this balance out of kilter and many parents are stressed and burnt out. They have put all their energies into caring for and attending to their children, so much so that there is little time and attention for themselves. While their intentions are admirable, the long-term results are bad for themselves and their children. If you are stressed and burnt out, you can no longer be there for your children; you can even become negative, inconsistent and resentful in your parenting. So you really have to turn this around and start with yourself.

The first suggestion we give to stressed parents is that they try to turn some of the care and attention that they have lavished on their children towards themselves. We suggest that they take time to identify and think about their own needs and wants, and then decide to prioritise and care for themselves as well as their children. The irony is that such a switch to self-care benefits their children as much as themselves, as the children will have access to more content, positive and resourced parents than before. Most of this book is about ways of providing positive attention and care to children and teenagers, whether this is by praise, encouragement, rewards or respectful listening and communication. The first step, however, is to make sure we treat ourselves the same way!

Build On Your Strengths As A Parent

You will notice that throughout this book we encourage you to build on your children's strengths and abilities. We also encourage you to apply the same principles to yourself. Too often parents give themselves a hard time, criticising their own behaviour and putting themselves down. Too often they focus on what they do wrong in every situation: 'I wish I hadn't lost my patience like that' or 'I should have more time for my children'. Similarly, parents can relate negatively to each other, focusing on what the other has done wrong: 'I don't like the way you interrupted me talking to the kids' or 'You shouldn't have lost your temper'.

We encourage you to break this negative pattern and reverse it. Start looking for what you and your partner are doing right as parents. Be on the lookout for the small steps of improvement you make each day, the times you manage successfully. Begin to notice what you like about yourself as a parent. Don't be afraid to praise yourself: 'I'm pleased at how I was firm in that instance' or 'I'm glad that at least I tried my best'. Equally, if you are part of a couple, be on the lookout for examples of behaviour you like in your partner: 'Thanks for supporting me like that' or 'I'm really pleased that you came home early and we have some time to ourselves'.

It is in your children's interests for you to identify your own strengths and successes. Children learn a powerful lesson from you when you model self-encouragement. They learn how to be confident and successful and how to relate positively to other people.

Often parents go through difficult periods when it is hard for them to be consistent or to give their children all the time they deserve. At times like these, the worst thing parents can do is excessively blame themselves or be over-defensive. It is better to try to learn from the experience, acknowledge what needs to be done differently and move on. Self-compassion is as important as compassion towards others. It is powerful modelling for children to see their parents being honest about their mistakes and not dwelling on them but moving on to make a fresh start. This helps children learn how to move on from misbehaviour in the same way.

Remember, the goal is not to be a perfect parent or to have a perfect child. Such people do not exist (and if they did they would be unbearable to be around!). Rather, the goal is to be a 'good enough' parent – someone who accepts themselves as good enough, appreciates their own strengths as well as their weaknesses, tries their best and learns from experience.

Who Is This Book For?

This book is for all parents who want to learn how to help their children grow up into happy, secure, well-adjusted and responsible adults. It is particularly for parents who are dealing with challenging behaviour problems and other childhood difficulties, who want a toolkit of well-researched ideas on how to solve childhood problems and encourage good behaviour in children. The ideas are drawn from the Parents Plus Children's Programme – a dvd-based parenting course on managing behaviour problems and promoting learning in children aged six to eleven, developed in the Mater Hospital Child and Adolescent Mental Health Service in Dublin. The book particularly focuses on the needs and issues facing parents of school-age children (six–eleven), though the ideas are relevant for younger and older children. There are corresponding books that particularly focus on the needs and issues of preschoolers (*Parenting Preschoolers and Young Children*, Veritas, 2005) and adolescents (*Bringing up Responsible Teenagers*, Veritas, 2001).

How To Use This Book

This book is divided into two parts. Part 1 outlines nine basic principles that provide a step-by-step guide to solving childhood problems. The principles are both preventative and positive and together they build one by one into a comprehensive toolkit that helps form good habits of positive parenting, which can be drawn upon when faced by any childhood problem.

Part 2 considers fifteen typical childhood problems and issues that frequently occur for children aged approximately six to eleven. Each chapter considers one of these problems in turn and shows how the basic principles from Part 1 can be applied to solve them.

There are a number of ways to read this book. You can systematically start at the beginning and read through each chapter from beginning to end, or you can start with a problem in Part 2 that most concerns you, and then work your way backwards to the principles and steps in Part 1. It is also possible to read one principle at a time and to apply this at home, before returning to the book for the next principle. The key to making the ideas work is to test them out at home.

Part 1

Nine Steps to Positive Parenting and Positive Discipline

Step 1
Pressing the Pause Button

Paula found the morning routine with her children, Suzie, 8, and Robert, 6, really pressured and stressful. It would start with the children refusing to get out of bed and Paula having to shout and literally drag them out of the bed. Robert would then dawdle getting dressed and Suzie would refuse to have breakfast. Robert would then try to watch TV, getting really annoyed when Paula would turn it off. Paula found herself having to cajole and coax the children along every step of the way, and it would always end up in a row with everyone being late.

When faced by a conflict or a difficult situation, we can find ourselves immediately reacting in a certain way, without too much thought or deliberation. Sometimes our immediate reactions are helpful; for example, when we naturally respond to soothe a child who is crying in distress. But other times they can be unhelpful; for example, if we overreact to a minor challenge from one of our children or if we say something damaging in the heat of a row. Many different things determine how we react to other people and our children. It can be simply a habit (good or bad) that we have developed over the years or it can be a repetition of how we were treated by our own parents in the past, or it can be to do with how stressed or strongly we feel about what is currently happening. In addition, we all have our specific weaknesses; we all have our 'buttons' that, when pressed by others, make us fly off the handle. Problems can occur, however, when we get stuck in our reactions or when they become over-rigid and negative. Most problems in families are maintained by patterns of reactions between parents and children that have become fixed over time. The problems continue to happen with parents and children reacting the same way with the same negative result for both of them.

In the example above, each morning is stressful for the family. But each morning the parent reacts the same way (cajoling and arguing with her children to get up) and each morning the children react the same way (dragging their feet) and each morning ends with the same result (a row and a stressful start to the day).

Press The Pause Button

So how can you break these patterns of reacting? What can you do to stop the problem from happening over and over again? The first thing you can do is to pause and think about what is going on. Rather than reacting the same way each time (and letting your children press your fast-forward button!) you decide to press pause so you can understand what is going on and then choose a more constructive way to respond. Consider now how Paula paused and thought through how she wanted to respond to the problem she was facing:

When taking time to think about the ongoing problem with the morning routine, Paula realised that she had become hooked into a pattern of cajoling, arguing and taking too much responsibility for the children getting ready. She realised that the routine was not clear in the morning and that many of the problems started the night before with a late bedtime, resulting in the children (and herself) waking up tired and cranky. She realised that much of Suzie's refusal to eat breakfast was her looking for attention from Paula, who was too busy arguing with Robert.

To address the problem, Paula resolved to do a number of things:

- First, she would sit down with the children and talk through the importance of getting up on time and in a positive frame of mind, and then do up a morning routine chart with the children (starting with them going to bed at the correct time each night), which listed all the morning steps of getting ready and which included them sitting down together to have breakfast.

- Both children were given an alarm clock and it was explained that it would be their responsibility to get out of the bed in the morning. (Paula made sure the clock was placed on the other side of the room so they would have to get out of the bed!)

- Paula resolved that she was not going to shout at them to get up. Instead she decided she would open the curtains and remind them once and, if they did not get up in five minutes, then she would calmly remove the duvet (after first giving them the option of getting up).

- To assist Robert in getting dressed, she decided that she would help him get started and check how he was getting on (making sure to focus on progress) but that it would be his responsibility to complete it. If he was not dressed by a certain time, she would still leave at the necessary time and he would have to get dressed in the car.

- Paula also made sure to sit down with Suzie and eat breakfast with her, even if Robert was still getting dressed. She tried to make this time relaxing and to involve a chat in their time spent eating together.

- To help motivate the children to work as a team and get ready, Paula said they would get a point on the chart each day everyone was ready on time (and five points would mean a big family treat).

- Paula also reminded the children that if there was a day that they were not ready on time, then this must be because they were tired and the result would mean that bedtime the next night would be ten minutes earlier.

What is important in the above example is that the mother took time to think through how she wanted to respond and resolved not to react to the situation by shouting or cajoling the children. You may also have noticed that some of the solutions that the mother undertook were about what she could do when the children misbehaved (remaining calm, backing off, giving the children choices) – and others were about avoiding the problem in the first place and teaching them how to behave well (setting an earlier bedtime and doing up the routine chart with the children).

When solving childhood problems it is always important to have both a Discipline plan (how you will respond when the problem happens or the children misbehave) and a Prevention plan (to stop the problem from happening in the first place and to teach the children how to behave well). We will explore creating these plans in more detail in Part 2 of the book, when we examine several common problems.

Choosing a different response

Pressing the pause button is essentially about allowing you as the parent to remain in charge – you remain in control and you choose how you will respond. This is different than reacting in the same way and letting circumstances or your children's behaviour control you (pressing your buttons to get a reaction!).

Pressing the pause button is about not being stuck and repeating the same way of reacting every time, but instead breaking a pattern and being able to choose a different, more constructive way of responding. See the table on the next page for some specific examples.

Problem	Negative Reaction	Result	Alternative Positive Response
Child always says 'No' when asked to do something	*Parent reacts angrily and argues with child*	Child digs heels in Battle of wills ensues	*Parent pauses and does not react to confrontation* *Offers child a choice of doing what asked and a consequence*
Child badgers parent for sweets at the supermarket	*Parent gets frustrated and shouts at child for constantly asking*	Parent feels bad, gives in and child gets extra sweet	*Parent calmly gives child a choice – if you ask me again you will lose your treat – but keeps rule*
Getting homework done is a real battle every evening	*Parent sits over child to do homework*	Ends up in a row each day	*Parent backs off and gives child space, and periodically checks on progress – focusing on what child has done well* *Lets school deal with undone homework*
Child constantly worried and anxious about non-specific things	*Parent gets sucked into listening to and talking about child's worries all day*	Both parent and child exhausted by the worries	*Parent sets aside a specific 'worry time' each day when she listens to child about the worries* *At other times encourages child to talk about other positive things*

Pressing the pause button gives you a chance to 'pause' and reflect about your parenting and to decide what type of parent you want to be. It gives you the opportunity to decide to be a constructive and positive parent who is both loving and firm, patient and fair (as well as self-forgiving and compassionate).

Finding what works for you

By pausing and taking time to think through what was really going on during a problem situation, you can come up with a respectful response that has a good chance of working. Often this is simply a case of remembering principles that you know already and remembering what has worked for you in the past. While you can't control how your children will react, what you can do is change your own responses. And you will find that when you choose respectful and empowering responses, taking into account your own and your child's needs, you will begin to positively influence your children. In simple terms, your children will begin to change as you begin to change. It is important to remember, however, that nothing works all the time or for everybody or in every situation. For example, in some situations, ignoring a child's tantrum can cause too much distress and it can be better to adopt a more soothing or listening approach. What counts is that you take time to think through what works for you and that you are flexible enough to adapt and change if something is not working. You may have to 'press the pause button' several times before you finally work out how best to manage a problem!

Tips for Going Forward

1. *Think of a particular problem that occurs in your family. Take some time to think it through to understand what is going on. Have you become sucked into a negative way of responding?*

2. *What might be a more constructive way of responding that could make a difference? What has worked better in the past?*

Step 2
The Power of Positive Attention

Homework was a daily battle with seven-year-old Paul. He would dawdle and take ages to get started, and only when his father had been nagging at him. Then it became a major task in itself – he would complain that he couldn't do it (when his father knew he could) and call his father over (interrupting him getting the dinner ready) and he would have to constantly make sure that Paul did it properly. Most days he had to sit over him the whole time to make sure it got done. During this time, Paul's father could become really angry with him. Sometimes homework could take two hours, after which both of them would be exhausted. Quite often things would end up in a row.

There is an important rule in psychology –whatever we attend to or concentrate on tends to increase in frequency and significance. Whatever we notice, highlight and comment upon our children doing, they will tend to do more of it and the behaviour will become more significant for both parent and child. The strange thing is that it works the same way whether this attention is positive or negative. Any behaviour you praise and encourage will tend to increase, but so will any behaviour you criticise, give out about and punish!

In the homework example above, the father has become trapped in the pattern of providing negative attention during homework. Most likely, he is hooked into noticing what his son hasn't done, or focusing on the homework he has done incorrectly. His child has learnt that the way to get father's attention is to complain and to say he can't do it, or to dawdle. If he takes a long time to do it, he gains his father's attention for these hours (even though this is negative attention).

So how could the father break this pattern and instead turn it into a positive pattern. The key is to shift his attention and to make sure he mainly provides positive attention when his son is behaving well and doing his homework. Consider the following steps he could take:

- Rather than waiting to be called over when there was a problem, the father would go over periodically and comment upon what his son had done well, even if it was only something small: 'You made a good start on that writing' or 'Great, you've got your book out on the right page'.

- If his son called him over with a problem, rather than telling him what to do, his father could always ask, 'What have you done so far?' and praise his ideas. He would then encourage him to identify the next step and give him space to complete this.

- He could invite his son to call him over when he has completed something (not just when he has a problem): 'Ok, so you are now going to try one or more of the sums, call me over when you have tried one' or 'So you are now going to look for all the new words in the section – call me over when you have some'.

- At the end of each section of homework, he could praise all his ideas and ask encouraging questions such as, 'What have you learnt?' or 'What did you enjoy most about your homework?'

- Finally, the father could make sure that something that is a 'natural' reward for finishing follows the homework (e.g. playtime).

Catch Your Child Being Good

The best way to break a negative pattern is to shift your perspective and to go out of your way to make sure your children get lots of positive attention and encouragement whenever they behave well – this means catching your child being good.

There is no one right way to provide positive attention. What is most important is that it is personal and experienced as genuine by both parent and child. With young children, a simple pat on the head or a warm smile can be enough. For older children, you may want to specifically comment on the behaviour you like. For example, you could say, 'I see you've started your homework. That's good' or 'I'm really pleased to see that you've come in on time'.

It can be difficult to make this switch to positive attention, especially when you are not used to it, or if you have experienced a lot of difficult behaviour in the past. However, it can make a real difference if you give it a try and let go of any resentment from past misbehaviour. Consider the example of Robin below:

Robin had been involved in a lot of conflict with her ten-year-old son, more often than not on a daily basis. This usually started with him refusing to get out of bed in the morning, while she repeatedly called him, with increasing irritation. This normally ended in a screaming match, thus setting the scene for the rest of the day. Almost every interaction between them until the end of the day was hostile and negative.

When Robin first started a parenting course, desperate to change things, she couldn't imagine being able to find anything good about her son's behaviour to which she could pay positive attention. However, when she stood back a bit from the situation and observed her son, she quickly saw that there were many previously unnoticed aspects of his behaviour that she could acknowledge with positive attention. When he brought his cup over to the sink after breakfast she smiled and thanked him. When he let his younger brother play a computer game with him she said, 'It's very nice that you are being kind to your brother'. When he sat down to do his homework, she was able to comment positively on this.

Over time she began to see more and more things that she could praise and encourage, and she began to enjoy the change of approach and how it made her feel different. Her son's behaviour changed positively over a number of months and the relationship between them improved markedly.

If you are used to a lot of difficult behaviour from your child and feel there is little you can notice that is positive, a good way to get started is to spend some time thinking about the things you like about your child. You might want to recall the times they behaved well in the past (however long ago!) or times you enjoyed together and felt close. When you have pictured some of these things, write down one or two of them. When you've made a list, keep it in a safe place, and over the next few days look for further things your child does that you like and begin to note these down also. As you collect more and more examples of good behaviour, your attitude towards your child will change. Then, when you're ready, you can share some of your observations with your child. By now you are giving some really good, positive attention to them.

Focus On What You Want

Catching children being good is essentially about switching your focus to attending to what you want rather than what you don't want. Often parents are very clear about the behaviour they don't want in their children – fighting, whining, staying out late etc. – but are less clear about what they do want from them. Instead of your two older children squabbling and fighting all day, what behaviour would you like to see? Perhaps you would like to see them getting along better, or sharing, or playing quietly together. Catching children being good is about thinking in advance about what you want and going out of your way to notice this behaviour and make a big deal when it occurs. Remember also to catch yourself being a good parent. As I have said earlier, it is important to apply these positive principles to yourself as well as to your children.

Making a shift to consistently focus on what you want, rather than what you don't want, can make a real difference in your life, transforming your own sense of self, your relationship with your children and with your partner.

Positive Attention Can Divert Misbehaviour

Psychologists have found that much of children's misbehaviour is rewarded by the attention it receives. They have also found that a bout of misbehaviour often happens just after a period of good behaviour that has gone unnoticed. By attending to the good behaviour first you can give children the attention they are looking for and divert them from seeking the attention negatively. A good example of this comes from a time I was working with a mother and her seven-year-old son and four-year-old daughter. The mother was describing how her son was often aggressive toward his little sister, and this concerned her greatly. As she was speaking I could observe the children out of the corner of my eye and I saw how the girl was beginning to annoy her brother. She was trying to take the figures he was playing with and he was beginning to get upset, taking them back from her. It struck me that he was on the point of hitting out, so, rather than let this escalate, I went over to him and said, 'It can be hard playing with your little sister, but you're doing a good job, letting her have some of your toys'. He enjoyed the compliment, relaxed, and then said, 'Look Tina, you can play with these figures and I'll play with these ones'. In this way, a bout of misbehaviour was avoided, and the child was reinforced for sharing with his sister. Of course this tactic does not work every time, but it can be very powerful in diverting misbehaviour to notice the good (or slightly good) behaviour that precedes it.

Can Children Be Given Too Much Attention?

Children can certainly be given too much negative attention for troublesome behaviour. Children who are constantly pestering their parents – pulling out of them and whining – have learned that this way of behaving is guaranteed to get a response. Instead, providing attention to children when they are not behaving in this way, for example, when they are quiet, pleasant and doing what is asked of them, will, over time, bring about positive changes in their behaviour.

Some parents may be reluctant to praise ordinary behaviour or give a lot of positive attention, fearing it will make their children big-headed or that they might become dependent on the praise they receive. Research shows that children who receive much praise and encouragement – especially for ordinary and simple things – turn out to be more successful, confident and securely independent adults. When positive attention is genuine and sincere, it is very difficult, perhaps impossible, to provide too much.

Building Your Relationship With Your Child

Providing positive attention is the best way to build your relationship with your child. Positive attention can come in many different forms, such as:

- Setting aside time to play
- Praise and encouragement
- Special chats
- Going on a walk together
- Setting aside time to do an activity your child really enjoys
- Teaching your child something
- Letting your child teach you something
- Reading together at bedtime
- Affection and cuddles
- Caring
- Expressing positive feelings
- Listening to your child's news
- Keeping a promise to your child
- Soothing your child when they are upset.

What works for one child may not work for another. For example, it is important to have a daily chat with your child where you can listen to their news and what is going on for them. However, different times work for different children, such as just after school, during mealtimes, before bedtime, when doing an activity such as walking, or in the car on a journey. Find what works best for your child.

Putting Money In The Bank!

Your relationship with your child is a bit like a bank account. Any time you provide positive attention you make a deposit in the bank account and any time you do anything negative your make a withdrawal. The key is to make sure you are always making deposits in the bank account so that you never run out – you want to make sure that on a daily basis you have lots of positive time and attention so that during the hard times there is enough money in the bank for when you need to make a withdrawal!

Tips for Going Forward

1. *Make sure to spend 'special' time next week with your children (it may be having a good chat with them or simply enjoying each others' company).*

2. *Be on the lookout for good behaviour and make a note of it when you see it.*

Step 3
Play and Special Time with Children

One of the biggest things that has made a difference at home has been setting aside a daily time to play with my daughter. She has really responded to the positive attention and her behaviour has calmed down completely. It has also been great for me to see another side to her and to really enjoy her company. I have to say that we both benefit.

My five year old was very jealous when his brother was born and this made things really difficult for a while. What made a difference was simply setting aside 'our special time' each day, just before bedtime, when we'd read or have a chat. The important thing was, my husband would look after the baby and this was our time together uninterrupted. This really helped my five year old. He'd look forward to it and so would I.

The Value Of Play and Special Time For Children

One of the most important ways to provide positive attention to children and to build your relationship with them is to set aside regular times to play with them on a one-to-one basis. Spending time with children in this way has many benefits:

- Play promotes physical, educational, emotional and social development in young children. Through play (aside from having fun), they learn new skills and abilities, express feelings and learn how to get along with other children. It is extremely important for parents to take special time to play with their children.

- Playtime can be a relaxing and enjoyable experience for parents as well as for children. In fact, many parents describe these times as among their happiest. Good playtime is a reward in itself to parents, providing an often-missed opportunity to enjoy their child's company away from stress and conflict.

- Playtime brings parent and child closer. Children are more likely to open up to parents before and after playtime. With older children it is often during shared activities that they will reveal concerns or special interests they have. Parents can really get to know their children by spending special time with them.

- Child-centred play allows children to take the lead and make decisions. Children who experience their parents giving them control in play situations are more likely to have a sufficient sense of security to allow their parents to take control in discipline situations. When parents respect children's rules in play, children are more likely in turn to respect parents' rules in other situations.

- Child-centred play is the best way to bring on a child's development and to help them learn new things. When adults play with children in a responsive way, they help them learn new language, how to take turns and how to communicate appropriately.

How Best To Play With Children

When I first started to play with my seven-year-old son, it didn't go so well. I realised that I had certain ideas about what we should play together, such as football or more physical games. When I stepped back and let him lead, I realised he had more of an interest in crafts and making things. This was all new to me but I let go of my own agenda of how play should go and sat down with my son. I remember how delighted he was when I took an interest in what he was doing. I also learnt so much about him and his talent for crafts, and it brought us closer together.

While there is no one right way to play with children, there are a number of guidelines that can be helpful:

Set aside a special time

Perhaps the most important thing to do is to set aside a special time to play with your children. In a busy parent's schedule, this may need to be planned in advance and prioritised as something important and not to be missed. Play sessions don't have to be long to be effective. With young children (up to eight years of age) short, daily play sessions of fifteen minutes can make a real difference. With slightly older children, you might want to have longer times less frequently (two one-hour sessions weekly) based around an activity or hobby.

Spend one-to-one time with children

Special time works best if it only involves one child at a time. While this can put extra demands on parents with many children, there is no replacement for one-to-one time with another person, in terms of getting to know them deeply and building an enduring bond with them. Even if it means slightly shorter or less frequent special times, it is still best to have quality one-to-one times with your children. These are the foundations of good family life.

Follow the child's lead

In good playtime, children should be encouraged to take charge and make most of the decisions. Children have many other arenas in life where parents are in charge, so playtime is their chance to try out decision-making and to develop confidence. Parents can sit back and follow the child's lead, valuing and affirming their imagination and initiative. With young children this simply means letting the child choose the game or activity and how to play it. With older children it means involving them in the planning of activities and future special time. In both cases it is useful to take time to get to know what your children are interested in and to value and affirm their ideas first. With young children, this can be simply watching carefully what the child is doing and then naming or imitating it.

Encourage children in play

It's easy to fall into the trap of correcting children when they play. Out of a desire to teach children, parents can find themselves being critical, saying, 'Oh, that doesn't go there' or 'It should be done like this'. I suggest that for special playtime, you go out of your way to encourage children, looking for things they are doing right and showing great interest in their activities. For example, you can use lots of positive comments such as:

I like that colour you have chosen.

It was a good idea to turn it around that way.

You're really persistent in finishing this puzzle.

Essentially it is about being a good audience to children in their play, taking a great interest in what they are doing, getting down to their level, providing lots of eye contact and good body language. Using encouraging statements and kind comments helps children continue in their play and promotes a rewarding experience for both parent and child.

Choose interactive, imaginative activities

The best toys and play materials are those which stimulate a child's imagination and creativity. They don't have to be expensive 'educational' toys. We all see children who turn away from the expensive toy only to transform the box and wrapper into an imaginative castle!

The best toys allow children to be active and creative rather than passive (as with television viewing) and which allow parent and child to do things together. It is important to have toys that match a child's age and ability level as well as their personality. For older children, choose activities which emphasise cooperation and which allow you to interact with them. For example, going fishing is often a better choice than the cinema as it gives you more of an opportunity to talk and relate together. What follows are some suggestions for play and special time:

Good Toys and Play Materials

Younger Children	Older Children
Playdough, plasticine	Jigsaws
Blocks/Lego (any building or construction kits)	Construction kits/models (boats, planes etc.)
Jigsaws (for appropriate age level)	Paints/colours
Dolls/figures/puppets Tea set, tool set	Creative activities such as making a collage
Farmhouse, doll's house	Board games
Soft toys	Football
Dress-up box	Outdoor games
Paints, crayons, colours	Special activities (fishing)

Good activities for spending time with children

Essentially you are trying to find activities and regular hobbies that you can share with your children as a means of building your relationship and staying connected. Below are some ideas:

Watching favourite TV programme	Following a football team
Doing homework	Making something (e.g. a craft)
Shopping together	Walking, cycling
Playing cards	Camping
Playing sport	Doing a course together
Baking/Cooking	Fishing
House chores (fixing a bike etc.)	Working on the computer
Walking the dog	Caring for a pet together

Playing With More Than One Child

As well as setting up one-to-one time with your children, there are many benefits to playing with two or more children at the same time:

- It helps children learn to share and get on with each other
- It enables children to feel close and connected to one another
- It gives you a chance to guide and support a child in shared play
- It is good for family bonding.

In busy families with many children, it may be more practical to set aside joint playtime (though we still recommend planning for some one-to-one time with each child, even if it is less frequent).

How to play with two or more children

1. Sit in the middle of the children

(or directly opposite them) In this way you can give both attention and take control if need be.

2. Ensure each child has an activity that they want to do

This can be *Parallel play* (suitable for children of different ages or interests), whereby each child has chosen a different activity and you are in the middle supporting them OR *Shared play* (usually suitable for children of similar ages), whereby the children play the same game together, taking turns.

3. Share your attention

Make sure to switch attention frequently between the children, supporting them in their play and ensuring each of them gets plenty of attention.

4. Be a good audience/commentator

Take turns commenting and noticing each child e.g. 'Pete has the blue block, and Julie has the green block'. This helps guide the play and keep children focused on what is happening. It is a good way to teach children turn-taking e.g. 'Julie is now taking a turn, Pete is waiting (good waiting, Pete!) … now it's Pete's turn …'

5. Look for any times the children notice and connect with one another and comment on this
e.g. 'Oh, David is looking at Jean's colourful picture'; 'You gave Pete a brick; that was kind'. This is the beginning of teaching them the skills of playing with one another.

Have family special time

As well as individual special time between parent and child, special time for the whole family together is important. Like playtime, this can get lost in the busy weekly schedule and often needs to be prioritised and planned in advance. Families can set aside a special Sunday meal, or family trip at the weekends as a way of spending relaxed, fun time together.

I'd been worried for a long time about my ten-year-old daughter who seemed increasingly unconfident. I realised that I was very distant from her and she was growing up so quickly. So I made time to take up a hobby with her and to help her learn something new. She chose to learn how to play the flute (which was completely new to me). The two of us went to classes together. Funnily enough, she proved to be a better player than me, and much of the time she would be helping me with how to play. Ironically, the fact that she was teaching her Dad rather than the other way round proved to be real boost to her confidence. I learned that I didn't have to 'teach' her anything but just be with her.

Listening To Children

Listening is probably the most important way of giving children positive attention. Setting aside regular times to listen to children, encouraging them to talk about their news, their feelings and concerns has lots of benefits. Listening is important because it:

- Builds children's confidence
- Helps children express themselves and understand their own feelings
- Helps children understand the feelings of other people
- Allows parents to get to know their children and to really get close to them
- Is the basis for helping children solve problems.

Active listening

Active listening involves paying full attention to what the child has to say, how they say it and the feeling behind it. It means the parent stops what they are doing, looks at the child and allows them to speak without rushing in with solutions, blame or sympathy. When the child has finished speaking, the parent repeats what they think the child has said and names the feeling the child seems to be showing.

The time for active listening

Active listening is valuable at any time, but it is not always practical for busy parents to abandon what they are doing so that they can actively listen to their children. It is particularly effective if used when the child has something exciting or upsetting they want to tell. Some parents find that by making a particular effort to actively listen to their children for maybe only ten or fifteen minutes each day they notice a big improvement in their children's behaviour and in their relationship with them.

Skills of active listening
Give your child your full attention
It is important to set aside a time when you won't be distracted and you can sit down and really listen to your child.

Go at the child's pace

Helping a child speak and express themselves may take time and patience.

Reflect back what the child has said

Simply by repeating what a child has just said or even just nodding can be sufficient in helping them go on and express themselves more fully.

Pick up on feelings

What distinguishes active listening from ordinary conversation is the concentration on feelings. Helping a child express feelings is crucial to helping them understand themselves and other people.

Tips for Going Forward

1. *Set aside a regular special time to play or spend special time with your children individually. For young children, this could be short, daily sessions of fifteen to twenty minutes. For older children, this could be less frequently but for a longer period of time; for example, in the form of a weekly planned activity.*

2. *During special time make sure to follow the child's lead, use lots of encouragement and, above all, have fun.*

3. *Establish a regular routine to have a chat with your child (e.g. bedtime, mealtimes), when you have time to listen to them.*

Step 4
Encouragement and Praise

I realised that I could be down on my children all the time, correcting them every time they did something wrong. Ironically, I was only doing it because I wanted the best for my children. I wanted to make sure they grew up behaving well and knowing right from wrong. But now I know that, while my intentions were good, I was on the wrong track. My children need my encouragement and praise much more than my criticism and correction. And this is the best way to teach them how to behave well. It is also the way I enjoy the most!

People often think that the best way to change a child's misbehaviour is to criticise and scold them when they misbehave – pointing out what they have done wrong and the error of their ways. However, being critical and negative creates many problems: criticism can damage a child's confidence and ability to change, it leaves both parent and child upset, and it gives attention to the misbehaviour.

Encouragement is a far more effective way to help children change, learn and grow. Rather than focusing on what is wrong, it is far more effective to encourage what is going well and to go out of your way to praise the examples of good behaviour you see. By becoming an encouraging parent in this way, you will notice an improvement in your relationship, as it is far more enjoyable and satisfying to encourage rather than criticise.

Often people think that children who have got into a habit of misbehaving or being 'bold' or 'naughty' don't deserve much praise or encouragement. The truth of the matter is that these children's confidence is such that they need encouragement far more than other children who are receiving it already. Helping these children see that there are some things they can do right is the best way to help them get back on the road to improved behaviour and better relationships.

Become An Encouraging Parent

Most parents agree with the principle of being an encouraging parent, but are often unaware as to how many of their statements are critical or negative. For example, suppose you saw your son being a little bit rough with his younger sister – you might respond with a criticism such as, 'Don't be mean to your sister' or 'Why are you always mean to her'. However, these statements are negative, focus the child on the misbehaviour and tell him he is bold (thus making him believe that). A more encouraging way to respond is to say something like, 'John, please be kind to your sister' or 'Listen, John, I know you can be a very kind brother to your sister, let's see some of that now'. This encourages John's positive qualities and is more likely to be effective. Look at the box below for some more examples:

Critical Parent		Encouraging Parent
Don't put that there	⟶	Why not put it here? / Let me show you
That's not right	⟶	Try it like this … good boy
Why are you always shouting?	⟶	Please use your nice voice
Don't fight with your brother	⟶	I know you can get on with your brother
You're doing it wrong	⟶	Oh, you are trying hard, aren't you
Don't get angry like that	⟶	I know you are upset at having to leave
Why didn't you pick the blue block	⟶	Oh, you picked the green block, you like green

Four praises to every criticism

Children need much more encouragement and praise than correction and criticism. This is especially true for children with behaviour problems. The golden rule is four praises to every criticism.

Skills Of Specific Encouragement

When we use encouragement or praise to promote good behaviour in children, we can make sure it gets through to the child by ensuring that it is clear, specific and personal.

Encouragement should be clear

You should have the child's full attention before you give encouraging statements. It is less effective to encourage with statements muttered under your breath from another part of the room or when the child is doing something else like watching TV and not really listening. It is important to get down to the child's level, to make eye contact and to use a warm and genuine tone of voice. The child should be in no doubt that they are getting a positive message from you. Think of encouragement as the most important message you can possibly give to your children. You really want to make sure it gets through to them.

Encouragement should be specific

If you want to help children to change positively, they need to know exactly which behaviour they are being praised for, and which qualities you are encouraging in them. Vague statements such as, 'You are a great boy' or 'Good girl' don't tell a child what you are pleased about, and can soon wear thin and seem insincere. It is more effective to say, 'Thanks for putting out the bins when I asked' or 'It is great to see you sharing with your sister'. These statements help children know exactly what good behaviour you are praising and make it more likely to occur again. It is also important to praise as soon after the desired behaviour as possible so they are in no doubt that it is that behaviour you want to see again.

Encouragement should be personal

The best way to encourage is unique to each parent and child. What is essential, though, is that your child experiences your encouragement as personal and genuine. Saying how you feel and expressing this to your child can make a real difference. Often this can be achieved by using an 'I' message. For example:

I really appreciate the way you cleaned up your room.

Thanks for coming in immediately when I asked you, that means a lot to me.

I really enjoyed playing with you today, I love it when we get on so well.

It is also very important to be affectionate when encouraging children, especially when they are younger. A simple hug or a pat on the back can speak volumes. Remember, what works in encouragement varies from parent to parent and from child to child. Find out what works for you.

Exceptions/Steps In the Right Direction

Often parents say that they never witness examples of the good behaviour they want in their children. For example, the children never do what they're asked, or they never share with other children. When you are feeling negative and angry, it can be hard to notice the positives. However, if you closely observe your children you will notice that there are always times, however short-lived, when they are behaving more positively. If you are serious about helping your children change it can make a real difference to notice these exceptions. Children need to know there are some things they are doing right before they can have the confidence to change.

It is important not to wait for perfection or a finished task before you encourage or praise. Change can be gradual, and, to ensure that children don't get demotivated, it is important to encourage and praise steps in the right direction. For example, encourage a child when she starts to do her homework: 'I'm pleased to see you sitting down straight away and starting your homework.' You don't have to wait for the homework to be completed. Encouraging the first step of a task helps a child persist and continue to the end.

Double Encouragement

The effect of encouragement can be doubled by involving other people. Praising a child in public or in front of important people can make it more powerful and really drive the message home. For example, if Dad has witnessed good behaviour, as well as praising it himself, he can double the impact by telling Mum about it in front of the child later in the day. There is often a tendency to nag about misbehaviour, to really focus on what is wrong. Using encouragement, you can turn this around and really go on about what your child has done right. Tell them repeatedly and everyone else of anything they have done that you are pleased with.

Persist With Encouragement

Many children initially reject encouragement and praise. They might shrug it off, saying, 'Of course I didn't do it right' or they may not believe the parent is genuine. If a child has not received much encouragement in the past, it can take a while before they can begin to accept the positives you point out. Equally, if encouragement is a new approach for parent and child, it can feel awkward at first and, like any skill, it can take a while before it becomes second nature. It is important not to give up if a child initially rejects encouragement. See this as a sign that your child needs the encouragement all the more. Persistence can really pay off.

Think about new ways to get your encouragement through. It might be a case of picking a better time or choosing different things to praise. It might help to change your style of encouragement to ensure it is clear, specific and personal. This all helps the child experience it as genuine. With older children it can be effective to sit down and talk about what it is you are pleased about and what it is you want from them. You can even explain your new positive approach, saying you want to have a better relationship with them and you believe that positive encouragement is the best way.

I found it hardest to start encouraging my nine-year-old son. I think it was because I had been critical of him for so long. He was a little suspicious of my intentions at first. He would say, 'You are just saying that to me because you want me to do something' or 'Don't try that stuff from the parenting class on me'. Things changed when I sat down with him and explained that I realised that I had been very negative in the past and I wanted to make a change, that I wanted things to be happy between us and wanted to be positive. Slowly he came on board and it began to work. One benefit that surprised me was how he became very encouraging and positive back to me.

Be Encouraging Towards Yourself

You can only be truly encouraging towards your children if you are encouraging towards yourself. In my work I meet many parents who for many reasons find it hard to be positive towards their children. When I listen deeper, I discover that they were never encouraged as children and in fact often experienced negative childhoods. In many cases, these parents have taken on board the negative messages from their childhoods and are extremely self-critical, always putting themselves down. Things only change when I can help that parent find a way of being more forgiving, accepting and encouraging of themselves. As the mother in the next example states, this change helped both her and her child:

With my youngest child I'm sad to say that I found it really hard to encourage her. I think it was because she was born at a difficult time in my life and things didn't go well from the start. Initially, all I could see was the negatives in her personality and the many behaviour problems I had with her. This was really hard for me as a mother as I thought I should be having only positive feelings, and I used to feel guilty. Change happened when I shared these feelings in a parenting group and realised that I was not alone in having them. As a result I stopped giving myself a hard time for having negative feelings. I was able to forgive myself and let go of my resentment. This freed me up to begin to appreciate the good things my daughter brought into my life. When I stepped back I began to notice lots of things I liked about her presence in my life. I began to understand her and was more able to be really positive towards her. The encouragement helped us both.

Tips for Going Forward

1. *Think of two qualities you like about your children that you will tell them next week.*

2. *Make a list of the behaviours you want to encourage (for example, getting along, sharing, playing well together).*

3. *Write down how you will specifically encourage any signs, however small, of these positive behaviours.*

4. *Be encouraging of yourself. What things are you proud of as a parent?*

Step 5

Establishing Good Routines

Most of the problems we had in our house stemmed from the fact that the children had a poor bedtime. They had gotten into the habit of going to bed late, and this left everyone tired and cranky. Once we devised an early and relaxed bedtime routine, things really changed. It was hard work at first, but really worth it.

The Power Of Good Routines

One of the keys to creating a happy household is establishing good daily routines with your children. In fact, many childhood problems are caused or made worse by poor or inconsistent routines in the home. For example, it is very common that children with behaviour problems have poor bedtime routines. As a result they tend to go to bed late. This makes them overtired and less likely to settle. In addition, their parents, who have often stayed up trying to get their child to bed, are also likely to be tired. This means that once the morning comes, both the child and the parents are tired and more likely to be irritable and fractious.

As a result, many problems can be avoided or at least made a lot easier if good, regular routines are established in the home. For example, establishing a regular and early bedtime for a child will ensure both child and you as their parent are rested and relaxed. (A good bedtime routine, which includes a relaxed reading time with you as their parent, can also be a real boost to your relationship.) As a result, behavioural problems and tantrums over the next day are less likely.

Examples of important routines to establish in your home are:

- Bedtime
- Morning routine
- Homework and coming in from school
- Chores routine (can be weekly routine).

Creating A Good Routine

Break the routine down into small steps

The first step is to sit down and think through what an ideal routine would be for you. Then break down the routine into small, clear steps that tell the child exactly what you want to happen. For example, a bedtime routine could be:

- TV/play outside from 6pm to 7pm
- Supper at 7pm
- Pyjamas and in bedroom by 7:30pm
- Reading with parent at 7:30pm
- Lights out at 8pm.

Make sure a 'natural' reward occurs at the end of the routine

Try and ensure something rewarding happens at the end of the routine. For example, reading when in bed, playtime after homework, TV after doing household chores.

Explain the routine to your children in advance

Sit down with your children and go through the steps of the routine in advance. Involve them as much as possible and let them make as many of the decisions as possible (what book they might read in the bedtime routine, or what subject they might start with in the homework routine).

Put the routine on a chart

Putting the routine on a clear chart can be very helpful. The more attractive the chart is, the better – some parents use photos on the chart to remind the child of what is expected (e.g. a photo of the child reading or asleep). It can also be really helpful to involve the child in making the chart with you (e.g. letting younger children colour it in etc.). This really is motivating for them and helps them take ownership of the routine. Figures 1, 2 and 3 (pp. 46–8) are examples of reward charts.

Consider using an extra reward to get the routine started

It can be useful to use an 'extra reward' to get a new routine underway. For young children, getting stars or stickers on a chart can be enough to motivate them; for example, they earn a star if they beat the timer getting dressed or are in their pyjamas by 7pm. For older children, a points chart can work best whereby the child earns points for good behaviour such as completing household chores. These can be turned into rewards at the end of the week (such as getting a dvd or choosing dinner).

The trick with children is to make the rewards you normally give them dependent on good behaviour and cooperation. For example, you may have the habit of giving children a treat at the weekend, but you could make them earn this through helping out with household chores. When children work hard for something they want, they learn to appreciate it more and it teaches them about responsibility.

Rewards don't have to be expensive to be effective. Even older children can be motivated by ordinary treats like extra playtime, a special trip etc. It is important to put some time into thinking which rewards will work for your child. It often helps to ask the child what they would like (within limits) to motivate them further.

Examples of good rewards are:

- staying up later
- special time with parents in the evening
- an extra bedtime story
- going shopping with a parent
- a trip out to the park or playground
- taking out a special toy that is not used frequently (e.g. the paddling pool in the garden)
- a trip to a favourite restaurant

- going to the cinema
- choosing a dvd at the weekend
- having a friend over to tea
- 20 cent extra pocket money.

Start small and be patient

Good routines take time to become established – especially if your children aren't used to them or are unfamiliar with the workings of an ideal routine. This often means starting with a routine that is easier to establish and then progressing to a more difficult routine when you have the confidence to tackle it, such as in the bedtime example below:

- Suppose your child goes to bed at 10pm and you want this to move to the better time of 8:30pm
- Rather than switching immediately to 8:30pm – likely to be very hard – do this gradually
- Sit down with your child and explain that you are moving to an earlier bedtime of 8:30pm and you are going to do this gradually
- For the first night he has to be in bed by 9:55pm, the second night by 9:50pm
- Give your child a small reward for each night he makes the target (e.g. 5 cent a night extra pocket money which he can spend at the weekend).

Be encouraging

Being positive and encouraging is really important in making routines and rewards work. For example, if you are helping your son learn to dress quicker (and beat the timer), as well as providing a star when he does it, be really encouraging as you go along. For example, when you see him trying, say things like, 'You are doing well, you have got your trousers on, only your jumper to go now – nearly there'.

Establish A Weekly Routine

It is also useful to establish weekly routines to ensure important family events get done and to ensure everyone takes responsibility for chores. Weekly routines can be created with children as part of a family meeting and can be altered as necessary as part of ongoing planning time with children.

A weekly routine can include things like:

- Family night
- Night out for parents
- Family trips
- Visiting relations
- Children's sports / activities
- Special parent–child activities.

Tips for Going Forward

1. Identify a routine that you want to work upon at home.

2. Divide the routine into small steps.

3. Do up a chart with the steps described in a clear pictorial way.

4. Make sure the routine ends with a rewarding activity.

Fig. 1

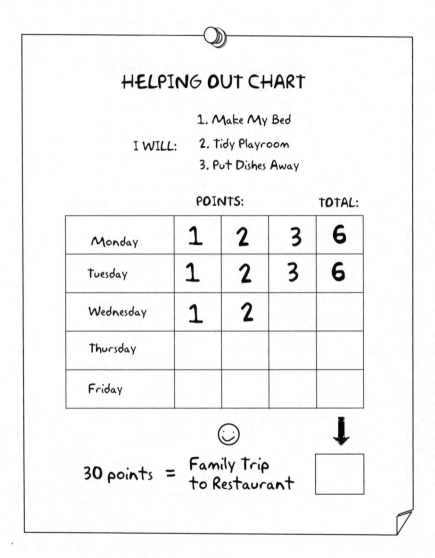

HELPING OUT CHART

I WILL:
1. Make My Bed
2. Tidy Playroom
3. Put Dishes Away

POINTS: TOTAL:

Monday	1	2	3	6
Tuesday	1	2	3	6
Wednesday	1	2		
Thursday				
Friday				

30 points = Family Trip to Restaurant

Fig. 2

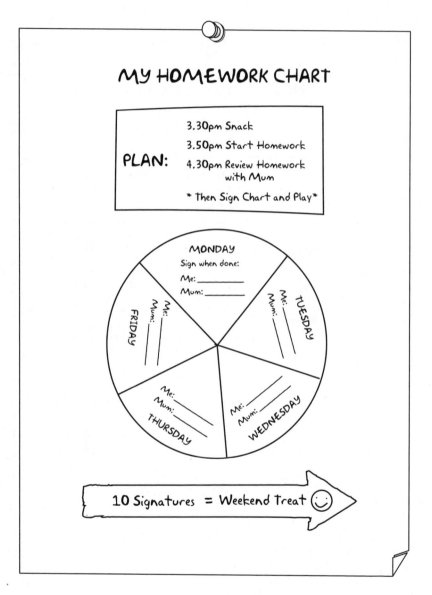

Fig. 3

Step 6
Setting Rules with Children

Getting The Balance Right

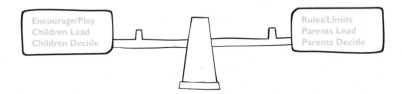

Just as children need parents who are loving and encouraging, so they also need parents who are prepared to set rules and limits. Good parenting is about achieving a balance between supporting and encouraging children to make decisions for themselves and setting rules and making decisions for them. Parents rightly feel obliged to teach their children good social behaviour. While it is important to teach children to think for themselves and to be self-responsible, it is also important to set certain rules and limits and to correct them when they step outside these boundaries. You may wonder what the best way is to do this. How can we set rules and limits with children in a way that teaches them self-responsibility? In addition, when we have set rules, what is the best way to ensure children keep them, or learn from the consequences if they don't? These are the questions we will attempt to answer in this chapter.

How Many Rules To Have?
Encourage children to make as many decisions for themselves as possible
Depending on their age, encouraging children to make many decisions and choices helps them to be independent and to grow up confident and responsible. Many parents create unnecessary rules and lose the opportunity to let children decide about different things. For

example, does a parent have to decide what colour socks her five-year-old wears? Does a parent have to decide what toys a child chooses in play? Do the grown-ups always have to decide what the family has for dinner? Of course the decisions children can make and those that a parent must make for them depend very much on their age.

Try to give children some choices
Give children choices even when you are imposing a rule or limit. For example, you may insist a child does her homework when she comes in from school, but you may give her choices about when and where she does it, provided it is done well. Or you may insist a child eats vegetables with his dinner but let him choose (within reason) which vegetables. Or you may insist a child goes to bed at 8pm but give her choices about the routine prior to going to bed. By giving children options within the limits you set, and by negotiating these with them, you increase their cooperation and self-responsibility.

Keep the rules you insist upon with children to a minimum
Keep the rules you set with children to a minimum, confining them to those that really matter. When children are demanding or oppositional, one of the errors parents can make is to try to take control by imposing many rules. However, too many rules often leads to more conflict, which in turn reduces even further the amount of time children cooperate with their parents' wishes. For this reason it is best to keep rules to a minimum, and focus only on the rules that really matter to you. Once these are chosen, it is important to work hard to ensure that your children comply with them.

Core Rules
Core rules are the rules that are the most important for your children to keep. These rules are non-negotiable and your children need to be helped keep them at all times. Core rules should be kept to an absolute minimum – and should only involve things like:

- Safety – e.g. wearing a seat belt, not going out late at night
- Education – e.g. homework must be done
- Health – e.g. medicine must be taken, children must go to bed on time to be rested
- Respect – e.g. speaking politely (no shouting or aggression).

The Golden Rule – Respect

The last core rule – respect – is one of the most important rules of all. During behaviour problems it is often the one most broken and the one that parents often let their children away with. Yet this is one of the most important rules to insist upon and to help your children keep.

However, if you insist upon the rule of respect for your children you must be prepared to keep it yourself. The deal is that you must aim to speak with respect at all times to your children. Children learn more from how you behave than what you ask of them.

Communicating Rules Respectfully And Assertively

People often fall into the trap of communicating rules and issuing instructions to children either aggressively or passively, rather than assertively. With aggressive instructions, we are more likely to use an angry voice and intimidating body language. However, this can be ineffective, resulting only in the child getting angry in return. Even if the child does what we ask, they are likely to be hurt or resentful and less likely to comply in the future.

With passive instructions we use a soft, whispery voice, hardly gaining the child's attention. In this case the child is likely to ignore what we say or not carry out the request because they feel we don't really mean it.

With assertive instructions we insist on gaining the child's attention by getting down to their level, establishing eye contact and cutting out distractions. We use a calm, polite and assertive voice, while keeping our body language friendly but firm.

Assertive instructions are not only the most respectful for both parent and child, they are also by far the most effective way to help children cooperate and do what we say. Learning how to communicate assertively takes a lot of practice, as often we are not aware of what our body language is communicating. Sometimes people communicate with a glaring expression on their face or a trembling in their voice but are unaware of this. Role play is one of the best ways to practice, either in a group where you can get feedback from other participants, or at home in front of a mirror where you can observe yourself. (You might want to make sure no one else is in the house at the time!)

Use positive instructions

As an experiment, I want you to consider the following instruction. I want you to not think of a blue kangaroo. Don't think of a blue kangaroo!

Were you able to carry out this simple instruction? On average, most people find it impossible to carry out a negative instruction like this because, to understand what is being asked, you have to visualise a blue kangaroo. Giving negative or 'don't' instructions to children creates the same problem. If we say 'don't' to a child – for example, 'Don't run in the shop' – the child has to visualise the forbidden action (running in the shop) to understand what we mean. Such an instruction immediately focuses them on the behaviour we don't want and acts almost as a suggestion to carry it out. In addition, 'don't' instructions only tell children what they can't do (something they often know very well!), and nothing about what they can do. With 'don't' instructions we give few ideas to children about how to behave correctly. Equally, we are more likely to give 'don't' instructions angrily, and this sets up the expectation that the child is about to misbehave. For this reason I suggest you issue only positive 'do' instructions to children. All negatively framed instructions can be made positive. All 'don'ts' can be turned into 'dos'.

For example:

'Don't grab the toys from your sister' can become 'Please ask your sister to share the toys'.

'Don't shout in the house' can become 'Please use a quiet voice in the house'.

'Don't hurt your little brother' can become 'Please look after your little brother'.

Make sure your request is clear

When parents ask a child to do something, they often muffle what they say or use vague language. Sometimes they don't even look at the child when they ask something. I remember one parent who used to shout many of her instructions to her children from another room! It is best if you make your requests very clear to your children. This means getting down to their level, using a firm but polite tone of voice, ensuring you have their eye contact and that they understand exactly what you mean. With young children who are preoccupied in something else, this can mean kneeling down beside them, getting their attention and making sure they are looking at you before you tell them what you want.

Give children time to comply

One of the biggest mistakes that parents make is that they don't give children time to comply with an instruction. They bunch instructions together and may have given three or four before the child has had a chance to carry out the first one. This leaves the child confused and burdened, and this invariably leads to conflict. When you ask a child to do something, I suggest you wait about five seconds before you issue another instruction or before taking disciplinary action. It can be helpful to count to five silently in your head. This helps to diffuse the situation and gives children time to decide how to comply.

Warnings and reminders are also helpful to children. For example, when children are engrossed in play before bedtime it can be helpful to remind them of bedtime by saying, for example, 'You will have to get ready for bed in ten minutes'. This gives children time to prepare and make choices about how to end their play.

Be encouraging

Being encouraging and supportive makes a big difference to helping children do what you ask and to keep rules. You never have to be angry or coercive; instead, an encouraging tone of voice can often work best. For example:

Listen, John, let's get these toys tidied up; it will only take a few minutes and then you can go outside and play.

It is also useful to acknowledge a child's feelings, especially when they are upset and finding it hard to keep a rule:

Look, John, I know you are upset, but I need you to speak politely.

Acknowledging a child's feelings does not mean you are giving in. For example, you can say to your child, 'I know you are upset at having to leave the playground and go home now', and then still insist the rule is kept and the child does have to go home.

Praise cooperation

It is important to get into the habit of praising children when they cooperate with your wishes. Commenting positively each time they do what you ask takes any 'power victory' out of the experience, and helps children see being cooperative as rewarding.

Often parents don't feel like thanking a child when they do something they are told, or they feel it is something the child should do anyway without praise. However, the problem with this approach is that behaviour not rewarded soon disappears. If parents wish to encourage their children's cooperation, thanking them when they do what they are told can make all the difference.

When–then instruction

A simple instruction which gets great results for parents is the when–then instruction. This is a positive instruction which orders events so that children experience a 'natural' reward following the completion of a task or chore. For example, you can say, 'Paul, when you do your homework, then you can watch TV'. Paul is given the choice of doing his homework and then having the reward of watching TV, or the choice of not doing his homework and having the consequence of not watching TV. Other examples are:

When you do your homework, then you can go out to play.

When you get ready for bed, then Mummy will read you a story.

The instruction can also be rephrased using the words 'as soon as'. For example:

You can have some dessert as soon as you finish your dinner.

You can watch TV as soon as you get dressed.

Tips for Going Forward

1. *With your children, write down the most important core rules of the house.*

2. *Make sure to use only positive instructions – Use DOs instead of DON'Ts.*

Step 7
Responding to Misbehaviour

I found the children's misbehaviour really hard to deal with because I simply did not know how to respond in the moment or get them to behave. This meant I was more likely to react angrily, which made things worse. Taking a step back and thinking through a clear plan of action in advance made a real difference.

When faced with misbehaviour – children refusing to do what they are told, being abusive or throwing a tantrum etc. – the temptation is to respond angrily and to punish the child using our anger and criticism. As discussed earlier, this approach is problematic: it provides attention to the misbehaviour, can provoke an angry reaction from the child, and if it becomes an ongoing pattern it can damage your relationship with your child. In this step we propose a different way of responding to misbehaviour, which involves pressing the pause button and using consequences as a means of disciplining the child (instead of punishing the child with our anger) and helping them learn to behave in the long term.

Pressing The Pause Button
Pressing the pause button means being able to unhook from negative interchanges and being able to calmly choose your response. It is about not letting the child's behaviour 'press your buttons' and control how you react. Instead, you remain calm and in control. This could mean not getting drawn into rows or screaming matches, but instead remaining calm, sitting out a young child's tantrum, or not responding to a child's nagging, calmly getting on with a job despite a child's whining or calmly walking away from an older child's excessive protests.

Pressing the pause button means you are in a position to discipline your child in a calm, constructive way.

Disciplining Your Child Using Consequences

We can not force children to behave or do as we ask. All we can do is offer children a *choice* between doing what we ask and a *consequence* for not doing so. The goal is to make it rewarding for them to take the choice we suggest and have an unrewarding consequence when they don't. The ideal is that the consequence is fair and just and helps the child learn about the negative implications of misbehaviour so that they can make positive choices in the future. Good discipline is really about setting up choices and consequences for children from which they can learn.

Logical consequences

Consequences work best when they are 'logical' and related to the misbehaviour. This helps the child learn to behave the next time. Examples include:

- If a child doesn't eat at mealtime, no food is made available until the next mealtime, even though the child is hungry (the child learns to eat at mealtimes).

- If the child stays off school (possibly feigning illness), then they stay in bed for the day (the child learns it is not fun to stay off from school).

- If a child comes in one hour late, then they have to be in one hour earlier the next evening (the child learns to come in on time).

- If a child gets aggressive during playtime, then playtime ends (the child learns to play appropriately).

Planned consequences (explored in more detail in Step 8)

Planned consequences (such as doing a Time Out, losing TV time or pocket money) work well with children and are useful in situations where there are no obvious logical consequences:

If you don't calm down now, you will lose some pocket money/TV time/computer time.

(When two children are fighting) *If the two of you don't calm down and get on now, you will both have to go to your rooms for ten minutes.*

Giving Children A Choice

Central to making consequences work is to ensure that they are given as a choice to children. For example:

You either play with the sand and keep it in the box or the sand gets put away.

You can either calm down now and play the game or the game will stop.

By being offered a choice, the child is given the opportunity to behave well and it is by *being aware that they are making a choice* that the child begins to learn to take responsibility for their actions. Essentially, by giving the child a choice you invite the child to 'pause' and to weigh up how to proceed. Just as you are pressing the pause button to unhook from a negative interchange as parent, giving the child a choice of a consequence is inviting him to press the pause button also – this is what makes the whole discipline system work.

Making Consequences Work

Remind children of the behaviour you want

Prior to using a consequence, make sure to give the child a clear request of the behaviour you want:

John, I want you to tidy the toys away now please.

Even when you offer a choice, the key is to make sure you keep the focus on the behaviour you want. Rather than saying, 'If you keep messing now, you will lose TV time', it is more effective to say, 'Come on, let's get these toys tidied away and you won't lose any TV time'.

Consequences only have to be small to work

Insisting your child is grounded for ten minutes can be as effective as being grounded for the whole day. Also this means the consequence is over quickly, giving the child a chance to behave well again. It also means that you have further options and can reapply the consequence later if needed (keep the child grounded for a further ten minutes).

Ensure consequence affects the child and not you

A mistake that parents make is to pick a consequence that affects the parent more than the child. For example, you might say to the child, 'If you don't behave now we will cancel the visit to Granny', only to realise that it is you and not the child who wants to visit Granny! So make sure to use consequences that affect the child and not you.

Plan consequences in advance

It is hard to think of consequences during a discipline situation when you are under pressure and likely to be feeling upset and annoyed. Under these pressures you are likely to pick a consequence that is too severe, or too hard to carry out, or one that simply will not work with your child. For this reason, it is really important to plan consequences in advance – sit down and think what consequences are best for your child in each problem situation you are likely to encounter.

Never run out of consequences

Always have an extra consequence up your sleeve. Think through what you will do if your child does not behave after the first consequence. Make your consequences small enough so you never run out. Instead of losing a TV programme, why not ten or even five minutes of it. This means you can repeat the consequence (and dock the child another five minutes) and are less likely to run out.

Always be respectful

Choices and consequences work best when you are respectful and calm and even encouraging:

> *C'mon John, I don't want to have to take away any more pocket money; let's calm down now and behave.*

Enforce consequences calmly

The essential thing about enforcing consequences is that it is a time for *action* and not *words*. It is best if a parent follows calmly and firmly through with the consequence without reasoning or scolding. Things can be talked about at another time.

Use extra consequences if your child continues to misbehave

Consequences can be chained together to form a plan of action. Think through what further consequences you can offer your child if they continue to misbehave, or keep the last consequence:

> *For each minute that you refuse to go to your room, you will have to spend a minute longer there.*

> *Every time you fight you are going to lose more TV time.*

Creating A Step-by-Step Discipline Plan

By chaining consequences together you can create an effective discipline plan that gives you a step-by-step action plan as to how you will deal with a particular problem behaviour. It helps you think through all the 'what ifs', so you will know how you will respond in most circumstances, no matter how your child reacts to your initial discipline. Consider the following problem:

Step-by-step action plan – TV and homework

Problem behaviour – Child refuses to do homework and turns the TV on instead.

1. Give child a clear, positive and assertive request:
   Paul, please turn off the TV now and do your homework.
   Pull back and wait to give child a chance to comply.

2. If child does not comply, give him the choice of a consequence:
   Paul, you can either turn off the TV yourself or I will. Which do you prefer?
   Pull back and wait to give child a chance to comply.

3. If child refuses, enforce consequence – parent goes and turns off the TV. (It is useful to have a 'what if' plan of action, thinking through what further consequences you will use if your child continues to misbehave.)

4. If child turns the TV back on, offer further choice:
   Paul, if you don't turn the TV back off now, you will lose TV time after homework.
   Pull back and wait to give child a chance to comply.

5. If child refuses, take action and turn the TV off again, but this time remove the plug/turn off the fuse.

Notice how in between each step it is crucial to pull back and wait – this shows the child how to 'press the pause button' and it gives him a chance to choose to behave well. By emphasising that they have a choice, you help your children learn how to take responsibility for their actions.

Remain Calm

Pausing and unhooking from angry ways of dealing with misbehaviour and instead using consequences and choices requires a great deal of self-awareness and effort on the part of parents:

Pausing and not reacting to my son's complaining and whining about his dinner was one of the hardest things I learnt to do. I think it was that I took it all personally. If he was saying horrible things about the food, it would really bother me. I'd try to ignore him for a bit and then I would give in and then argue and cajole him. I realised the fact that I finally caved in and gave attention was making things a lot worse. Things changed when I was able to not let things get to me. For example, instead of arguing when he complained about the food, I would simply say in a matter of fact way, 'You don't have to eat it if you don't want to, but there won't be any more food until next mealtime' and then get on with my own dinner and chat with the rest of the family who were enjoying the meal. When I stopped arguing, his complaining stopped. He still tested me later, asking for a snack before the next meal, and I'd respond, 'Oh, no snacks now, but we will all be having dinner at six'. He would then complain and argue, but I simply remained calm and got on with something else. At the next dinner he did eat his meal. I must say I was tempted to gloat, 'Now, don't you see that I'm not trying to poison you, it is good food', but I bit my tongue, and ensured I was positive, telling him I was delighted to see him trying his food. This new approach really worked, though it was hard in practice.

Tips for Going Forward

1. *Think of a behaviour problem that is happening at home.*

2. *Identify consequences for this misbehaviour that you can use with your children.*

3. *Remember to offer your child a choice between behaving and experiencing the consequence.*

Step 8
Planned Sanction Systems

For some problem behaviours there are clear consequences that are fair and logical. For example, if a child is getting aggressive with a toy, then the toy can be put away until he calms down, or if two children are fighting over the TV remote, the TV can be turned off until they sort out the disagreement. In both these cases the consequences are related to the behaviour and can appear fair and will make sense to the children. There are many problem behaviours, however, where there are no obvious consequence (such as defiance, abuse, aggression etc.) or when the behaviour happens so frequently that you run out of consequences.

In these situations, it is a good idea to set up a sanction system in advance that allows you to always have a consequence no matter what problem behaviour you encounter and no matter how frequently the behaviour happens.

There are two main types of sanction systems that parents can use, both of which provide a parent with a discipline system that allows them to be in control and which is respectful of the child:

- Privilege Loss – docking the child pocket money or TV time when they misbehave.

- Time Out – sending the child to their room or another venue such as the hall for a short period (e.g. five minutes) until they calm down.

Principles Of Sanction Systems
What age do children have to be to use a sanction system
Privilege loss works with children once they are able to understand the concept of a choice and to link the loss of privilege to the problem behaviour. Children from as young as three years can be

helped understand the system (if it is explained very well using pictures and a chart) and it can work with children as old as sixteen (once the privilege loss is carefully selected to be meaningful). Time Out generally works best with younger children (three–seven years) and can become problematic with older children if they refuse to partake. However, if parents use a back-up privilege loss system ('if you don't go to Time Out now, you are going to lose pocket money') then it can be adapted for older children.

Explain the sanction system in advance

The key to making a sanction system work is to make sure that you think through the system and plan it in advance. You also need to sit down with children in advance to explain the new discipline system. It is important to be positive about the purpose; for example, you might explain that it is about helping them to get on better together, or learning better ways of resolving disagreements other than hitting out. Explain that it is about helping everyone – children and parents – learn how to speak calmly and respectfully to one another (the golden rule), to calm down in angry situations and avoid rows and shouting which might otherwise occur.

Involve all children in the new system

Whatever sanction system you opt to use, it is very important that you include all your children in the system. It is not fair to target one child as this is likely to make them feel excluded, increase sibling rivalry (see Part 2) and make the problems worse. Instead, all children should be included in the system, which is explained as a way of helping everyone get along and communicate respectfully to one another.

Making A Privilege Loss Sanction System Work (e.g. Pocket Money)

In order to make a 'privilege loss' discipline system work, you need to identify a privilege that is small and repeatable and which you can use frequently and daily without running out. TV time and pocket money are two good examples, with pocket money being the most versatile. Below, a possible pocket money sanction system is described.

Setting up a pocket money sanction system

How much money?

Decide on a daily amount of pocket money for each of your children. Try and make this correspond to what they get from you normally. For example, if you give them €7 a week pocket money then the daily amount is €1. Or if you give children weekly and daily treats amounting to €5, then the daily amount is 70 cent (and you stop providing treats and let them buy them with their own money). When starting to use this system, many parents say that they don't provide pocket money, but when they count up all the treats their child gets, it can amount to €15 or €20 on a weekly basis! The key is to make these treats and this money dependent on your child behaving well – your child has to earn their pocket money. This will teach them responsibility.

How many sanctions do you need?

Decide on how many sanctions you are likely to need on your worst day and divide the money accordingly. (For example, if you feel your son could misbehave twenty times a day, then the sanction amount should be 5 cent, which allows you to use the sanction twenty times in a day.)

Give the pocket money at the same time each day

Allocate the money at the end of the day and start afresh the following day with a new amount e.g. at a chosen time, give your son the pocket money, saying something like, 'You earned 80 cent today. You lost money for shouting and being rude, but you still got 80 cent. I hope you will get the full amount tomorrow'.

Implementing the pocket money sanction system

Sit down and explain to your children in advance about the system

As detailed above, explaining the sanction system in advance and in a positive way is crucial to getting your children's cooperation and making sure they understand it.

Give your children a warning before giving a sanction

In some cases you might have to issue a sanction without a warning (e.g. if a child hits out or is abusive), but the ideal is to always use a warning and to give the child a choice to behave well.

If you shout again you are going to lose pocket money.

Each minute you delay getting ready for bed you will lose pocket money.

As with all consequences, it is the choice that makes the discipline work and which teach the child to act responsibly.

Never run out of sanctions

Make sure to never run out of pocket money sanctions in a day, otherwise your child will have nothing to work for. If you find yourself running low, slow down in your delivery of the sanctions (try and pull back from the conflict).

Remain calm throughout

The system will only work if you remain calm and always respectful.

Let the sanctions do the work, not your anger

When your child misbehaves, instead of getting angry or shouting, use the sanction system.

Step-by-step action plan – pocket money sanction

Problem behaviour – Child acts out and starts shouting.

1. Remind child of rule / State what you want to happen:

    John, please speak politely.

    Pull back and wait to give child a chance to comply.

2.   Give child a warning:

If you don't speak politely you will lose pocket money.

Pull back and wait to give child a chance to comply.

3.   If child ignores warning, issue sanction:

You have lost some pocket money.

Pull back and wait to give child a chance to comply.

4.   Remain calm and firm and do not give into child.

5.   Repeat as needed:

Please speak politely; if you continue to shout, you will lose more money.

Using Time Out As A Sanction

Like a pocket money sanction system, Time Out works best when it is thought through in advance and then explained to the children.

Setting up Time Out
What behaviour?

Children need to be absolutely clear which behaviour will lead to Time Out (e.g. hitting out, breaking things). Parents should stick to this and not include other behaviours in the heat of the moment.

Where?

Children should know where Time Out will take place. This ideally should be a safe place where there are not too many distractions. A hallway or bedroom is often used. The Time Out place should not be a scary or unsafe place such as a shed or a bathroom where medicines are kept.

How long?

Research shows that Time Out only needs to be short (about five minutes) to be effective. It should not be longer than ten minutes, unless the child continues to make a fuss. *The essential rule is that children need to be quiet for at least two minutes before they can come out.* This means that if they protest, shout or scream, they will have to stay there longer. The goal of Time Out is to interrupt negative behaviours and to help children learn self-control and how to calm down. If they are let out while they are protesting or are still angry, this defeats the purpose.

Step-by-step action plan – implementing Time Out

1. Misbehaviour occurs.

2. Parent gives warning if appropriate:

   If you throw another toy you will have to go to Time Out.

   (For some behaviours e.g. hitting, a warning may not be appropriate and the child should immediately go to Time Out.)

3. Misbehaviour occurs again, so parent insists child goes to Time Out.

4. If child refuses, the parent adds on minutes to Time Out period to a maximum of ten minutes (e.g. 'That is six minutes for arguing').

5. If child continues to refuse, parent offers choice between Time Out and a back-up sanction:

   Right, you either choose to go to Time Out for ten minutes or you lose X (a back-up sanction like TV time) *... it's your choice.*

6. If child refuses, Time Out is dropped and the sanction is enforced.

Ending Time Out – flow chart

7. The parent ensures child stays in Time Out for the selected period or until the child has been quiet for at least two minutes. It is important that the parent does not give in to the child's protests or screams, otherwise they will learn that the way to get out of Time Out is by protesting.

8. If the child refuses to come out of Time Out at the end of the time period, the parent simply ignores this and makes no comment.

9. When the child comes out of Time Out the parent does not criticise or nag about the misbehaviour but is upbeat, offering the child a suggestion of new positive behaviour (e.g. 'Do you want to go and play now?'). The misbehaviour has now been dealt with.

Using back-up sanctions to make Time Out effective

Time Out is essentially about giving a child a choice. If parents resort to dragging their child to Time Out, it is self-defeating. The crucial thing is to help the child *choose voluntarily* to go, thereby helping the child to learn self-control and take responsibility. Having a back-up sanction makes Time Out workable in most situations. Most children when faced with the option of Time Out and the loss of a privilege will choose Time Out.

Children Fighting Against The Discipline

Once you start to impose a discipline system, many children will resist and do everything they can to get you to give up the discipline and to get their own way. This is especially the case for problem behaviours such as abuse or aggression, in that if it has been going on for some time, the child is likely used to being in charge. Some children can employ a whole range of negative tactics to get you to stop disciplining them:

• **Emotional blackmail:** For example, saying, 'You are really mean'; 'You don't love me' or worse.

• **Attacking the system:** 'I don't care, keep all your money, I don't want it'; 'If you think that is going to work, you are stupid.'

• **Being aggressive and abusive:** shouting, throwing a tantrum (making you feel they will keep it up until you give in).

• **Using threats:** 'If you don't give me the money, I'll hit out / hit my sister / break something.'

Think through how you will respond

The key is to anticipate your child using these tactics, and to see it as normal. Then you can think through how to respond. It is crucial to:

- Remain calm, positive and assertive
- Not give into your child's demands
- Impose consequences if need be, but generally pull back and not get hooked into your child's misbehaviour.

Plan of action

It is also useful to have a plan for how you will respond to each of your child's negative reaction – a sort of 'What If' plan:

- If my child continues to shout I will give him a choice: 'John, if you continue to shout you will only lose more pocket money.'
- If my child badgers me, I will say, 'John, keep your distance please'.
- If my child follows me, I will get up and leave the room and go about my business.
- If my child gets aggressive, I will assertively say, 'John, keep your hands to yourself' and pull away (I may impose another consequence later for this).
- If my child threatens to break something, I will say, 'Now John, if you do that you will just have to clean it up later/pay for it'.

Be Patient – Sanctions Take A While To Work

Sanction systems are not miracle cures and can take time to work. As discussed above, some children can initially resist them and instead increase their problem behaviour to get you to change your mind. However, once you don't get 'hooked in' and remain calm, positive and firm – not giving into your child's negative demands – then over time these tantrums will reduce. It is important to remember that by being firm and not giving in, the intensity of the tantrum you are currently dealing with may increase, *but the number and intensity of future tantrums will reduce.*

We found Time Out hard to implement in our house with our six-year-old son. Often the Time Out itself would end up as a battle of wills and was becoming counter productive. When we reflected on it we realised that we were making a number of mistakes. First, we hadn't really talked the idea through with our son to explain it to him and to gain his cooperation. Second, we were implementing it in a bit of an authoritarian manner and were probably arguing too much with him as we sent him to Time Out, rather than saying little, being calm, persistent and firm. To remedy this, we sat down away from the problem and talked through with him the reason for Time Out. By listening to him we realised that he disliked the fights as much as we did, but also felt that we were doing as much of the shouting as he was (this challenged us to reflect carefully about our own behaviour). We then explained a more positive reason for Time Out, that it was literally a time for all of us to take a break from a situation and to calm down. We explained that it wasn't because we didn't love him or that he was a bad child, but that we really did love him and just wanted to find ways for everyone to get on better. In addition, we decided to emphasise his choices (about giving up the misbehaviour when warned, or about choosing to go to Time Out or getting another sanction). We weren't going to force him anymore. This talking it through with him really helped make Time Out more cooperative. It could still be difficult to implement, but we realised that much of the challenge was in controlling our own responses, ensuring they were calm and respectful.

Tips for Going Forward

1. *Think of ongoing behaviour problems happening at home for which you might use a sanction system.*

2. *Identify what sanction might work best with your children (e.g. Time Out, loss of pocket money or TV time etc.).*

3. *Explain the system to your children in advance and gain their cooperation.*

4. *Write down a step-by-step plan as to how you will implement the sanction system.*

5. *Expect your children to resist the sanctions and think through how you will respond calmly and firmly no matter what happens.*

Step 9
Problem Solving with Children

When I had a blow up with my son, I found it really helpful to come back and talk through the issues later with him, when we were both calmer. Then we could speak politely and civilly to one another. I could listen to his point of view and he could listen to mine and we could think about ensuring the row didn't happen again.

Just as in this book we have encouraged you to 'press the pause button' in order for you to reflect about your own feelings and actions, so it is also important to help your children learn to pause and reflect also. The most effective long-term way to help children behave well and be responsible as they grow up is to help them express and understand their feelings and to think through the consequences of their actions. You want to help them learn how to respectfully communicate and to discover solutions to problems that take into account their own feeling and needs as well as those of others. The best way to do this is to make sure you have plenty of time to talk and particularly to listen to your children, both when things are going well and when problems arise.

The 'techniques' described so far to manage behaviour problems, such as positive rules, consequences and planned sanctions, only work in the long term when children have time to reflect on their actions and to discover new ways of behaving. This helps children to understand their own feelings and those of other people, to think through the consequences of their actions and to discover positive alternatives to misbehaviour which are good for them and other people. Often a good way to do this is to set aside time to talk to your children both on a one-to-one basis and also as a family together during family meetings.

Talking Problems Through

Talking things through can be divided into different stages:

1. Setting time aside
2. Listening to one another
3. Thinking up solutions
4. Agreeing a plan.

1. Setting time aside

Often parents make the mistake of trying to talk a problem through with a child at a time of conflict. As discussed in previous sections, what is called for at these times is withdrawing attention from the misbehaviour, helping children learn by experiencing consequences for their actions, and maybe a cooling-off period for both parent and child. Generally, it is better to talk problems through with children away from the conflict situation at a different time when everyone has calmed down. It is a good idea to set up a particular time to sit down with the child when you both won't be distracted and which doesn't conflict with anything else (don't select a time during your child's favourite TV programme). In addition, try and allow a bit of time for problem-solving sessions, as talking things through with children can take time. Rushing can preclude either parent or child from being heard and may lead to conflict.

2. Listening to one another

Listening is probably the most important communication skill of all. When we truly listen, we step out of our own shoes and into those of another person. We try to understand the world as they see it, not just as we see it. Such listening is a great service to others as we all need to be understood. Being understood by another person helps us to understand ourselves. Active listening is very important to children. As well as being the best form of positive attention, it helps them understand their thoughts and feelings and those of other people, as well as bringing parent and child closer together.

Yet listening is also probably the most difficult skill of all. Most of us have no training in it and it requires a lot of effort on the part of the listener, especially when there is conflict between the listener and the person being listened to. Children in particular are often not listened to. Their thoughts, feelings and viewpoints generally aren't seen as being as important as those of adults. Instead of listening, parents often fall into the trap of giving advice, criticising, or coaching – all useful skills at times but not when we are actively listening in an attempt to understand a child's feelings. Consider the following responses to a child:

Paul (upset):   James grabbed the computer game from me.

Parent: Well, you shouldn't have being playing with it for so long (criticism); or Why don't you play with something else? (advice); or Oh, don't worry, it's not so bad (coaching); or Let me go and talk to James (rescuing).

Active listening involves giving children your full attention. It involves setting aside anything else you are doing to really concentrate on what they are saying (verbally and non-verbally). Perhaps the two most important aspects of listening are: a) reflecting back to children what they are saying so they feel understood, and b) acknowledging their feelings. Consider now some alternative listening responses:

Paul (upset):   James grabbed the computer game from me.

Parent: Sounds like you are upset. Sit down and tell me what happened (sensing the child's feelings and encouraging the child to say more); or Poor you, I know how much you like playing that game (acknowledging the child's feelings).

In the above examples, the parent is validating the child's feelings and attempting to see the problem from his point of view. Sometimes simply repeating what the child has said, or nodding encouragingly can be sufficient in helping the child feel listened to and encouraged to express more.

Sometimes listening and coming to a new understanding of how your child is feeling is sufficient in helping solve a problem. Consider the example below:

My six-year-old son used to be always acting the clown in front of other children and adults. It used to really bother me, because I thought he looked stupid and that people were laughing at him rather than with him. I used to feel embarrassed and would snap at him. I remember one time when he was upset, I sat down and listened to him, and he blurted out that he felt he could do nothing right, that everyone thought he was a fool. I suddenly realised that the reason he probably 'acted the clown' was to get the approval he desperately craved. More difficult to realise was the fact that I was part of the problem, by being critical and embarrassed by him. I resolved to get to know him differently, to believe in him as my son and to defend him against other people's criticisms.

Helping your child listen to you

As well as listening, it is important that, as a parent, you are able to give your own point of view, especially when you feel strongly about something or when it is an important discipline issue. But it matters a lot how you do this. Often people fall into the trap of blaming, or not acknowledging their own feelings. Good communicators acknowledge their feelings, express their positive intentions and focus on what they want. This is not only the most assertive and respectful way of communicating, it is also the most effective and the most likely way you will get your child to listen. Consider the following examples of Ineffective versus Effective Speaking Up:

Ineffective: You never do what you are told. You are really bold (over negative, over general, blaming).

Effective: Look, I want you to put the toys away now, as we are going to have dinner (clear request with a positive intention).

Ineffective: You are such an inconsiderate child, you always make me late (excessive blaming, damaging 'you' message).

Effective: I feel frustrated when you don't get up on time for school. You see, it makes me late for work and I need to get to work on time. I would like it to go a lot smoother in the mornings (clear 'I' message, parent focuses on what they want from the child).

3. Thinking up solutions

Once you have understood your child's point of view and expressed your own feelings, you are now in a position to think with your child of alternative solutions to the problems you are both facing. Rather than simply giving your own solutions, it is important to hold back and encourage the child to come up with solutions themselves. This can be done by asking questions such as: 'How do you think you can solve this?'; 'How can you ensure you get home on time?'; 'What other ways can you get a go on the computer without hitting out?' Though it may be tempting to come up with your own answers, it is crucial to proceed at the child's pace and to wait for them to generate the solutions. Children are far more likely to carry through solutions they have generated themselves. You will be surprised at how even young children, when given time, can come up with solutions which are as good as or even better than those thought up by parents.

It is important to help children generate as many alternative solutions as possible. Try not to be critical at this stage; encourage your child's creativity and listen to all the ideas they come up with. These can include solutions tried successfully in the past. For example, you son may remember that when he stayed away from certain boys in the class on previous occasions he didn't get into trouble. Once talked about and understood, these past solutions are more easily repeated.

I was surprised at how a problem-solving approach worked with my six-year-old son as I thought he was too young to think constructively. He used to get into big fights with his two-year-old brother, Sam, over sharing, and I used to jump in and 'solve the problem for them' and this would lead to tears. After pausing to think about it, I decided to handle things differently. Instead of jumping in, I backed off and simply asked him questions like, 'Oh, we have got only one helicopter and two boys wanting to play with it, what can we do?' or 'What can you give Sam to play with while you play with the helicopter?' Surprisingly he would often come up with good solutions such as 'We can take turns' or 'He can have the crayons while I'm playing'.

4. Agreeing a plan

Now it is time to help the child decide which solutions they are going to use. During this stage the emphasis is on helping children think through the consequences of the ideas suggested in the last stage, in order to identify those which have the best results, both for them and for other people. Frequently, children come up with unrealistic or inappropriate solutions. However, rather than criticising, you can guide them by asking them to think of the consequences. For example, as a way of getting to use his brother's computer, a child might suggest taking a turn without asking. But on thinking it through he realises that this could get him into more trouble if his brother finds out and then refuses to let him use the computer at all. A good question to ask the child is: 'Which solutions will leave everyone feeling happy?' (mum, dad and child, other children etc.)

Meeting again

When a plan of action is chosen, it is important to arrange a time to talk again to review how the child is getting on. Often things aren't solved immediately and you need to be there to support and encourage them.

Problem solving in action

To give an example of these four stages in action, consider the following scene of a father sitting down to talk to his nine-year-old son, who has hit another boy at school.

Active Listening

Father: You know I said earlier I wanted to talk to you about what happened in school.

John: It wasn't my fault, Robert started it (whining defensively).

Father (calmly): What happened exactly? (father does not get into a quarrel but listens to the child to hear his perspective.)

John: Well, we were out in the yard, playing football. Robert started teasing me so I hit him.

Father: It wasn't very nice of him to call you names.

John: No.

Father: You must have been angry (father picks up on his son's feelings and helps him feel understood).

John: Yes (nods), and then I got into trouble … Mrs O'Reilly sent me to the line.

Father: Sounds like you feel it was unfair, that you think Robert should have got into trouble as well? (acknowledges feelings.)

John: Yeah.

Helping child listen

Father: Do you know why Mrs O'Reilly sent you to the line? (father helps child think through the consequences of his actions.)

John: Because I hit him?

Father: Yes, and while I'm sorry you were called names in school, we have to find other ways of solving it than hitting out. I don't like when you get into trouble in school, because I want you to get on well and be happy there (father expresses his feelings for his son, his positive intentions and what he wants to happen).

Generating solutions

Father: Can you think of a way to handle it without hitting him?

John (thinks): I don't know.

Father: Come on, you're often very good at school, I am sure you can think of something (father points out that there are times his son behaves well in school, thus encouraging him to think of solutions).

John (thinking): I suppose I could tell him to stop.

Father: Exactly ... a perfect way ... can you think of anything else?

John: I could just walk away.

Father: You could just walk away ... anything else? (father is encouraging and positive about each of the solutions his child generates. He doesn't put them down or criticise.)

John: I could tell the teacher ... but she never really listens to me.

Father: I could have a word with her then?

John (thinks): I don't know.

Father: Maybe you want to think about that one (father lets child decide, thereby helping him to take responsibility).

John: Yeah.

Agreeing a plan

Father: Let's look at what ideas you've got. If Robert jeers at you again, you can just walk away or you can tell him to stop ... or you can have a word with your teacher or I could step in and have a word with her? (father summarises the solutions and helps child make a plan.) What one do you think is best?

John: I'll just walk away when he jeers me.

Father: That sound like a good choice. Sure we'll talk again tomorrow to see how you get on (father sets a time to review the plan).

John: OK, Dad.

Family Meetings

Family meetings made a huge difference to our family life. Organising a regular time when we could all be together, to talk things through, to plan things and just to have fun together really transformed things. We became much closer as a result and even when my children became teenagers they still made a commitment to be around on a family night.

Family meetings are an excellent way of solving family problems and preventing them from arising in the first place. By having a regular time to meet, you ensure there is always a time in the busy week where you can sit down to spend time with your children to discuss any important issues. They give you an opportunity to stay connected with your children and keep the lines of communication open. They can be used to talk together about important issues, have fun, make plans (such as for holidays), negotiate family rules (such as how much TV to watch, or who does the washing up) etc. Though they can be difficult to establish initially, family meetings can have a transforming effect. Many parents describe them as invaluable in completely altering the tone of family life from one of conflict and distance to one of cooperation and closeness. In addition, it is a good idea to establish the routine of family meetings when your children are younger, when they are much more likely to be open to them.

Tips on running family meetings

- Meetings work best if they are in the context of a 'family night' which involves other activities such as a family meal or a family game or another fun activity.

- Prepare for the meeting and make sure there is an agenda. As well as deciding what you want to raise as the parent, find out what your children want to discuss. The more you can make the meetings relevant to their concerns, the more involved they will be. A good way to prepare is to have a notice board in the kitchen to which children can pin things they want to discuss.

- Meetings run best when they are run democratically, with a special emphasis on trying to reach consensus or 'win–win' agreements. Though parents might initially lead, it can help to alternate the role of chair and give someone else the task of writing down decisions, and another person the responsibility of keeping track of time.

- Make sure everyone gets a chance to speak (even the very youngest) and a fair share of the time. The most important role you have as the parent is being a listener.

- Use the problem-solving steps above: listening, speaking up, thinking up solutions, choosing the best solutions etc.

- Don't be in any rush to solve things immediately. It can take a couple of meetings to solve problems and often the most important role is to hear and appreciate everyone's point of view.

- Write down any decisions and plans that are made and make sure to have a follow-up meeting to review how everyone is getting on.

In running our family meetings, the children would often bring up things that I didn't think were that important, but in hindsight I realise how important they were to them. On one occasion, my daughter put on the agenda how she didn't like her brother calling her names. When I listened, I was surprised at how hurt she was by this and it was great to see her articulating her feelings. Her brother, to his credit, was able to listen and also listed his own complaints, and in the end they reached an understanding. Though I wasn't involved directly in this problem, solving it in the family meeting brought us all closer together.

Tips for Going Forward

1. *When having a problem with one of your children, set aside some one-to-one time to talk it through with them. Remember to listen first, to speak assertively and to encourage your child to come up with some solutions.*

2. *Think about establishing a family night in your family. Maybe talk to your children individually about it and then call a family meeting to discuss the idea.*

Part 2

Dealing with Common Problems

Solving Childhood Problems

In Part 1 we described nine essential parenting principles and techniques that could be used to teach children responsibility, promote their learning, build self-esteem and ensure close, connected family relationships. The principles were a balance between:

- Positive Parenting (Play, Special Time, Listening, Encouragement) and
- Positive Discipline (Positive Rules, Routines, Consequences, Sanctions)

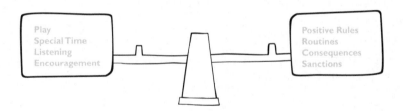

In Part 2 of this book we consider several common childhood problems and show you how to apply these ideas in different situations. First, let's recap on some general principles on how to solve childhood problems.

Take Steps To Solve Problems

Whatever the problem you are facing, it is a good idea to be proactive. Rather than letting it happen over and over again, take time to think through how you want to respond and to come up with a plan of action. Below are some steps you can take to reflect on and to solve childhood problems. You can use the steps by yourself or in discussion with a partner or another involved family member. As your children get older you can even involve them in the problem-solving discussion.

1. Pressing the pause button
Rather than reacting to a problem, pressing the pause button means taking time to stop and think about how you want to respond to a problem. This gives you a chance to remain calm and in control and to choose a positive response.

2. Think carefully about what is really going on during the problem
Is your child looking for attention or is she feeling inadequate? Is it a power struggle between the both of you? Is it caused by your own unrealistic expectations? For example, maybe the behaviour is pretty normal for a child of this age, or maybe it is understandable in the context of her special needs. During this stage of problem solving, it is important to take time to appreciate your child's point of view as well as being aware of your own feelings and reactions. Some honest self-reflection is called for.

3. Focus on your goal and what you want to happen
Rather than over-analysing the difficulties, a good way to approach a problem is to focus on the goal and what you want to happen, and to consider questions like:

- How do you want your child to behave?
- What does your child want?
- How do you want to respond as a parent?
- What skill does your child need to learn in order to behave well?

The last question is an important one, because a good way to think of misbehaviour and many childhood problems is to see that a child has not yet learnt the skill of how to behave well. For example:

- A child who is disruptive in class has not yet learnt how to keep the class rules of sitting in their seat, taking turns etc.
- A child who becomes emotional or hyper when something goes wrong has not yet learnt how to deal with frustration.

You can see it as your job as a parent to teach your child the skills of behaving well. If your child finds it hard to concentrate in tasks, think of things you can do to help them learn how to concentrate and what you want to achieve.

4. Come up with solutions and make a plan

At this stage, the important thing is to consider as many possible solutions as possible. Solutions usually divide into strategies and ideas for:

1. How to respond when the problem happens or when your child misbehaves.
2. How to stop the problem for happening again and/or how to teach your child to behave well in the long run.

When thinking up solutions, the key is to come up with a balanced plan of action that includes both prevention and discipline strategies.

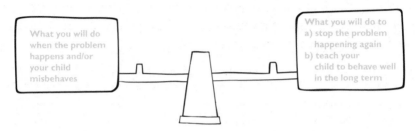

Discipline Plan

Prevention Plan

What you will do when the problem happens and/or your child misbehaves

What you will do to
a) stop the problem happening again
b) teach your child to behave well in the long term

In thinking up solutions, it is a good idea to remember what has worked with your child in the past, as this is the best way to discover what strategies are likely to work again. For example, one parent realised that it was a 'bad time' to harangue his daughter with questions about how school went the minute she came in and remembered that a better time was later, after dinner, when everyone was relaxed.

5. Review how you get on

Set aside a later time to review how the plan is working and to consider if any changes to it are needed. If something isn't working, try something different. For example, if a TV sanction is hard to work, maybe try pocket money instead. Or if your child is not responding to ignoring, then maybe try distracting them instead. While it is a good idea to make sure to give a plan a good chance to work, the important thing is to be really sensitive to how your children are responding to your plan. Be prepared to have to try out a few different responses or to think about the problem several times before you find what works for you and your child. In addition, nothing works all the time and, as children grow up, you may have to be flexible and change how you respond.

Problem Solving In Action

In the remaining scenarios we consider how to apply these problem-solving principles to a series of common childhood problems. In looking at each problem we first try to understand what is at issue for the child and then, where appropriate, we propose both a Prevention and Discipline plan to resolve the problem.

Problem I
Sibling Rivalry and Fighting

My son, who is eight, seems to be constantly picking on his six-year-old sister. We don't seem to have a day without her screaming that he has hit her and then me having to go in to separate them. I send him to his room when I catch him at it, but he still seems to be angry. Some days it can feel like they are fighting and squabbling all day long.

Sibling rivalry characterised by constant fighting and bickering is one of the most common childhood problems that parents face. Indeed, many other problems that parents identify such as a child being aggressive or having low self-esteem or constantly seeking attention are often best understood in the context of rivalry with brothers and sisters. Certainly many other problems are made worse if there is also rivalry going on.

At the heart of sibling rivalry is competition for parents' love and attention. Children are generally 'fighting' for their parents' approval and for their place in the family. There may be particular reasons for the rivalry – for example, one child might feel inadequate because his brother is getting on better at school. Or an older child might feel a little jealous of a younger child who is getting more attention.

Generally, sibling rivalry only becomes an ongoing or constant problem when the parent gets hooked into being a referee, sorting out the children's problems and deciding who is right and who is wrong. The strange thing though is that being a referee in this way generally makes the problem worse. The child judged by you to be at fault usually feels wronged and resentful towards you and his brother or sister, and is likely to restart the fight to seek justice. The child who was deemed to be right enjoys your approval and is likely to draw you in again in the same way (by crying or whining) to regain your support. Both children are likely to continue to involve you in the fight in order to win your approval and neither of them learns how to sort out the dispute by themselves.

In some situations, a pattern can build up over time, with one child being characterised as a 'problem' child who starts the fights and the other child being the 'victim' who can't stand up for himself. Both children live up to the descriptions and they can become self-fulfilling prophecies. It is easy as a parent to only see the same pattern – for example, you only see the older child picking on the younger one (but don't see how the younger one winds him up or deliberately annoys him when you are not looking).

The solution to sibling rivalry lies in *never taking sides in your children's dispute* (even when you feel one of them is wrong or has started the problem). Instead, you insist they sort out the dispute themselves, and if you have to discipline them for fighting, then ensure that it is always done *equally*.

Taking this absolutely fair stance is often hard for parents to do, so let's look at this in more detail from a prevention and discipline point of view.

Discipline Plan – Responding To Sibling Fighting

The following is a possible step-by-step plan for responding to a dispute or fight between your children.

1. Wait before getting involved

Rather than jumping in the minute a fight or dispute happens, it can be useful to pause and to give your children a chance to sort out the dispute themselves.

2. Remind the children of the good behaviour you want

If the children continue to fight, rather than criticising or refereeing, simply give the children a positive instruction asking them to behave well (see Step 6 – Setting Rules with Children):

> *Listen guys, I want the two of you to calm down in here.*

> *Please come to an agreement now and calm down.*

It can help to be really encouraging and to express a belief in their ability to get on:

Come on lads, I know the two of you can get on well together, let's see some of that now.

3. Problem solve

If the children continue to fight, one option is to support them in sorting out the problem. You do this by encouraging them to listen to one another and to come up with their own ideas and solutions.

OK, both of you want to play with the PlayStation, how can we sort this out?

Though problem solving in the heat of the row can be hard, it can work if you remain calm and don't get drawn into the row. It has the advantage of showing your children how to remain calm and how to resolve conflict.

4. Use an equal consequence

If the children continue to fight, you can also use an equal consequence. This is best offered as a choice and should always be fair and imposed equally.

Look guys, if you continue to fight, you will both have to go to your rooms.

Look guys, if I have to come in again, you are both going to lose some pocket money.

Over time, this fair approach removes the reason to fight – which is essentially a fight over your approval and attention. See Steps 6 and 7 (Responding to Misbehaviour) for more information on using consequences effectively.

Prevention Plan – Helping Your Children Learn To Get On And Sort Out Disputes

Problem solve together

To help your children get on, it can be a good idea to sit down with them together (at a good time when they're away from the original fight) and to help them sort out their disagreements. As a parent, your focus is on finding solutions rather than analysing who is wrong. Rather than being the judge or taking sides, start by saying what you want e.g. 'I want to help the two of you learn to get on more, so things will be happier in the house'. Then your job is to listen to both their points of view (and to help them listen to each other) and then to guide them equally to take responsibility for solutions e.g. 'What can you both do to make things go smoother between you?' The next step is to listen to your children and encourage them to come up with their own ideas to solve things. See Step 9 for more information on problems solving with children.

Problem solve individually

Sometimes it can help to talk the problem through individually with a child. Once again, the core principle is not to take sides or to collude with your child against their brother or sister (even though this child is not present). You can be sympathetic and listen to your child's feelings, but you don't make a judgement, and instead help them think of the other child's feelings and what can be done to sort things out. For example, if your daughter comes running to you complaining that her brother hit her, rather than rushing in to judge, you can be sympathetic ('I'm sorry that happened'), listen to what happened ('It sounds like you were both annoyed') and then help your daughter think of solutions ('What can you do the next time this happens?').

Equally, rather than lecturing an older brother that they should just get on with their younger brother, you can first appreciate his feelings ('It can be hard having a little brother sometimes when he seems to get all the attention'), help him understand his brother's feelings ('What do you think he feels?') and once again focus on solutions ('What can you do the next time you feel annoyed?').

The key in both the examples is not rushing to take sides, but instead staying impartial or, as I like to put it, staying on both your children's sides (and never supporting one over the other). See Step 9 for more information on problem solving with children.

Set aside one-to-one time with your children

Sibling rivalry can be really helped by ensuring you have regular one-to-one time with each of your children when you can appreciate their unique talents and personality and when you can enjoy their company and spend relaxing time with them. This can relieve them of the 'need' to fight for your attention and can work very well in situations where an older child is jealous of the younger child who appears to be getting all the attention. Setting aside a regular special time with this child, which is sacrosanct (and not interrupted by the younger sibling), can make a big difference in reducing jealousy. See Step 2 for more information on using positive parental attention in play.

Love your children uniquely

Competition between children is aggravated by comparisons. One child feels inadequate because the other is doing better at school or in sports or with friends. As a parent, it is important not to get drawn into comparisons but instead to appreciate the unique talents and interests of each of your children. You enjoy and appreciate one child's talent in music and the others in sport. If one child is feeling inadequate, the key is to find their area of strength and passion and to pay this the same amount of attention as you would the activities of the other child.

Set up shared activities between your children

Helping your children play together and work together as a team is one sure way to reduce rivalry and to help them bond together. You can do this by encouraging them to work together in a shared household task or by supporting them playing together. When you see any moments of sharing, be sure to notice this, saying, for example, 'You gave your brother some of your cars – it is good to see you sharing' or 'That was kind – you helped your sister out' or 'It is great to see the two of you working together as team'. See Step 3 for more information on playing with two children.

Problem 2
Homework Battles

Homework can take ages with my son. He dawdles and takes a long while to get started. Then he is easily distracted and won't apply himself. It's not that he does not know the stuff, because I know he can do it. I find I have to sit with him as he does each little bit, and even then it is a battle. Sometimes getting the homework done takes hours and we often end up in a row.

For many parents, ensuring a child does homework is a real battle, and the problem described above can become an almost daily event. Children struggle at doing homework for many reasons. Sometimes it is because:

- The material is too hard for them and the teacher is not sensitive to this
- They find it hard to apply themselves or concentrate on the task
- Some specific aspect of their homework is difficult for them (e.g. writing) and this has not been picked up in school
- Bad habits have become established and avoiding homework has become a pattern
- Homework takes a long time because it is a good way of getting Mum or Dad's undivided (albeit negative) attention.

When dealing with homework battles, it is worth taking a step back to understand what is going on and to consider what might be the issue.

Prevention – Helping Your Child Enjoy And Learn From Homework

Set up a good homework routine

A regular daily routine that incorporates homework helps build good learning habits, and it is worth taking the time to establish this:

- Create a quiet, relaxed place (no TV or distractions)
- Set a regular time for homework (e.g. after a short snack, when they have come in from school)
- Aim to do homework within a fixed period of time (e.g. half an hour) and have a maximum time (e.g. one hour) after which you will finish
- Have a 'natural' reward at the end of homework (e.g. playtime) with a strict rule that only when homework is finished can the child enjoy the reward.

It can help to write down the routine on a chart for your child and to go through the steps, especially if you are just establishing it. Having a special reward can be a good way of helping your child get used to a new routine. See Step 5 for more information on establishing good routines with children.

Be available to support your children as they do their homework

While it is always your child's responsibility to do the homework, it really matters if you take an interest and are there to support them. This involves getting to know what homework they have to do and encouraging them to talk about it.

1. Helping children get started

Help your children get started by listening to them describe what homework they have to do and then helping them plan how they are going to do it.

So you have Maths and English to do as homework; which would you like to do first?

2. Be there to encourage

It is useful to be nearby or available when your children are doing their homework so you can offer encouragement as needed (see Step 4). It can be useful to check in occasionally to offer support. The key to helping your children learn is to always first notice and affirm what they have done well.

That was great reading; you finished the whole page!

That word was tricky, but you got it.

You are nearly there, only half a page to go.

3. Check how your children got on

When your children have finished homework it is a good idea to check in with them and ask them what they have learnt and what they enjoyed.

You are finished your English – what did you read about? (Did you like the boy in this story? etc.)

What did you think about those sums?

What have you learnt?

What did you enjoy doing today?

Don't worry if your child does not have the homework done perfectly or if there are mistakes. Be wary about insisting that the child repeat homework that is incorrect, especially if it is going to lead to them being demoralised.

Consult With Teacher

For ongoing homework problems, do consult with your child's teacher. The teacher will be able to report on your child's performance at school and may have some ideas on how you can structure homework at home (e.g. some teachers agree that only a certain maximum time should be spent in homework and / or the child should take any uncompleted work to class). Talking with the teacher could highlight any special needs your child might have and together you can consider the best action to take (e.g. whether your child needs extra support and / or whether it is a good idea to seek an assessment for this).

Discipline – Responding When Homework Is A Struggle

Take a pause

If you find yourself getting angry and/or frustrated, the important thing is to take a pause and step back. Expressing your anger or frustration can only makes things worse as it may make your child dig their heels in and it certainly takes all the fun out of learning!

Give your child space

If you find yourself getting into an argument or pressurising your child to do the homework, it is a good idea to step back and give your child some space. Say something like, 'Have a read of the question, or try and read a sentence or two, and I will be back to you in a minute to see how you are getting on'.

If there is conflict between you and your child, consider taking a break from the homework. It is better that less homework is done rather than slipping into a negative pattern in your relationship with your child.

Give choices

You can't force a child to do homework – all you can do is set up consequences which make it rewarding for the child to have a go and try to learn. For example, if your child wants to stop homework you can say, 'Well, the rule is you have to try for a bit longer – there will be no TV until you at least try some of your maths homework'. Aim for small realistic goals e.g. ten minutes reading completed successfully rather than twenty finishing in frustration.

Let your child experience consequences for not doing homework

Remember, it is ok for your child to take incomplete homework into school, as this helps the child take responsibility and also lets the teacher deal with the issue (and see where the child is struggling). If you feel your child is not trying hard enough it is good idea that they experience the consequences in school. You can also set up consequences at home that encourage a child to complete homework e.g. a ban on TV until they have finished or at least shown they have tried their best, or a reduction in pocket money if the homework is not completed.

Supporting Your Child's Learning And Education

Aside from ensuring a good homework routine, and supporting your child while doing homework, there are a number of other things you can do to support your child's learning and education.

Work closely with the teacher and school

Children do best in education when parents stay closely involved in the school and build a good working relationship with their children's teachers. This means going to all parent–teacher evenings and school events, openly communicating with the teacher about difficulties and working with them regarding homework schedules and discipline issues as needed.

Encourage learning at all times

Aside from homework, try to encourage your child's learning in lots of other fun and enjoyable ways. The more learning is made interesting and enjoyable the more likely your child will succeed. You can do this by:

- Doing crosswords or maths puzzles
- Arranging a trip together to the library
- Reading books together
- Going on educational websites together.

Use everyday situations as opportunities for learning

Learning and education is happening all the time. Use everyday fun activities as opportunities to help your child develop curiosity and imagination. For example:

- As you cook dinner, ask your child to help you follow the steps in a recipe. Talk with them about the different ingredients and ask for suggestions and ideas.

- As you watch TV together, talk with your child about the programmes. If you're watching one of their favourite programmes, encourage them to tell you about the background of the characters, which ones they like and dislike and who the actors are.

To promote active learning, listen to your child's ideas and respond to them. Let them jump in with questions and opinions when you do things together. When you encourage this type of give-and-take at home, your child's participation and interest in school is likely to increase.

Problem 3
Oppositional, Strong-Willed Children

My six-year-old girl always says 'No' when she is asked to do something. It can be a daily battle to get her to cooperate with anything, and we often end up in a big row. It is so different with my two other children, who are really placid and cooperative.

Opposition, constantly arguing or refusing to do what parents ask is a common childhood problem. Whereas this behaviour is normal for two year olds who are discovering their own independent will as distinct from their parents, the behaviour can continue for children as they become older, and it can be more of a problem. Many children have strong-willed personalities which means that they particularly like to be in control and find it hard to be told what to do. Sometimes, the parent can also have these traits and this can lead to a clash of wills, which can result in endless battles. The classic pattern is as follows: the child refuses to do something, the parent reacts angrily and tries to insist the child does it, the child digs their heels in and a battle of wills ensues. Over time, if the behaviour pattern is repeated often enough, then the parent–child relationship can suffer and this can reduce cooperation even further.

Childhood opposition and disobedience also flourishes when parents are over-permissive and avoid setting rules with children. This gives children inappropriate control, leads to resentment between parents and children and does not prepare children for keeping rules in other situations such as school. The best parenting approach is a balance between insisting on important rules and encouraging children to make decisions (appropriate for their age) for themselves.

Prevention – Encouraging Your Child To Cooperate

Reduce rules to a core minimum

The key to encouraging children to cooperate is to keep your core rules to a minimum and to agree these in advance with your children (see Step 6). This should be kept to central things like safety and respect.

Establish good routines

As has been stated in many parts of the book, one of the keys to well-behaved children is to establish clear routines in advance with children (see Step 5). With children prone to opposition, this can avoid many problems as they know in advance what is expected and they get into a habit of behaving well. Rather than there being a constant battle about getting homework started, they get into a habit of starting when they come in from school. Or rather than a battle about choosing what clothes to wear in the morning, they get into the habit of choosing the night before.

Let children make as many decisions as possible

Children who have a tendency to oppose their parents value being given the opportunity to make decisions and this encourages their cooperation. Offering limited choices to children can encourage cooperation:

Marie, would you like to have peas or carrots with your dinner?

John, which homework subject would you like to start with?

Alice, which do you prefer to wear – the green or blue jumper?

Communicate rules positively and assertively

The way you ask children to do something is as important as what you are asking them to do. If you are angry or negative in your tone of voice, this can make a child defensive (especially a child who is prone to opposition) and less likely to do what you ask. The best way to ask children to keep rules is to be clear and positive, using an assertive tone of voice. See Step 6 for more examples on this assertive way of communication.

Teach children how to behave

Children who like to be in control appreciate being given responsibility for tasks and activities. In fact, this is often one of the strengths of their personality – they are willing to learn and take on responsibilities at an early age, and this can be a big boost to their confidence. You can use this to your advantage as a parent, taking time to teach them how to do chores and tasks that normally lead to conflict. For example, rather than continuously going through a big battle over getting your daughter to dress or do her hair in the morning, why not take time to teach her how to do these tasks herself, thus giving her the responsibility.

Model cooperation for your children

Cooperation is generally a reciprocal process. The best way to teach your children how to cooperate is to model appropriate cooperation with and for them. This means that you try to do what your children ask as much as possible – when what they ask is reasonable, something they can't do for themselves, and when they ask you to do it in a polite, respectful way. This means that you will politely refuse if your child asks you aggressively ('John, I can only answer if you ask nicely') or if it is unreasonable ('John, I think you can get your coat yourself'). But it also means you cooperate if your child asks politely ('Of course, John, I will get your coat, and thanks for asking nicely – that is good manners'). Complimenting a child on good manners makes it more likely for this behaviour to happen again and teaches them respectful communication.

Set aside one-to-one playtime

Setting aside a regular playtime with your child, when they can be in control and make the decisions about what to play and how to play, is not only a boost to your relationship with your child, but can also reduce the need for your child to be in control at other inappropriate times (when you, as the parent, are setting the rules) (see Step 3).

Enjoy your child's personality

Finally, children who are oppositional are often highly spirited and assertive. As with bringing up all children, it can be really helpful to focus on the positive aspects of your child's personality. Learning to enjoy and appreciate their spirit and many of their other positive qualities can take the sting out of conflicts and shift things to a more positive footing.

Discipline Plan – Responding To Opposition

Pressing the pause button

When faced with opposition, a good first step is to pause and take a step back so you can evaluate the best way to respond. Good questions are:

- Is it important to insist on what I want?
- Is this a core rule that is important for my child to keep?

Pressing the pause button is useful when faced with opposition because it stops you from reacting immediately. Sometimes, angry immediate reactions ('What do you mean you are not going to do it?') can fuel the row and increase opposition. If you take a moment and come back a little later, often your child will be more cooperative.

When dealing with oppositional behaviour, a key principle is to choose your battles wisely. Many rules that parents make for children are unnecessary and the situation can be handled in a different way. When you do state a rule, you must be prepared to follow through and insist your child keeps it.

Use consequences and choices

The best way to respond to childhood opposition is to think of a possible consequence for the child not keeping the rule or not doing what you ask:

- If you don't come in when I ask, you will have to come in earlier tomorrow.

- You will not be able to watch TV or use the computer until you finish your homework.

Using consequences in this way are described in detail in Steps 7 and 8. The essential aspect of this approach is to emphasise that the child has a choice to behave well and to deliver the consequences in a calm, respectful way.

Have a back-up plan of action

If opposition is a major issue, it helps to think through a discipline plan of action that outlines what you will do (in a step-by-step way) if your child refuses to keep a rule. Having a plan of action helps you feel in control and allows you to remain calm and respectful. In Step 7 a detailed plan of action is described for how to deal with a child refusing to turn off the TV and do homework. This illustrates how sometimes it is important to think through all the 'what ifs' of how your child might react – and in turn come up with an idea of how you will calmly and respectfully respond.

Problem 4

Hyperactivity, Impulsivity and Poor Attention

My six-year-old daughter is on the go all the time. She never seems to sit still. She is also having trouble keeping to the structured rules of the classroom.

My ten year old is just so impulsive – he never thinks things through. If you say, don't do something, he just seems to do it anyway – I can't get through to him.

Two-year-old and three-year-old children generally have poor attention spans and are often impulsive and very active, thus the reputation of the 'terrible twos'. Generally, as children get older they begin to quieten down and are more able to concentrate for longer periods and to pause and think before they act. However, for some children this improvement is slower in coming, and a small number retain impulsive, active and inattentive behaviours as they grow up. Children with these qualities are often harder to bring up and present special challenges to parents. These children often find it harder to comply with the structured environment in the classroom, which can lead to associated behavioural problems and poor self-esteem. Some of the difficulties these children have are sufficient to gain a diagnosis of Attention Deficit Hyperactivity Disorder (ADHD) and can benefit from specialist assessment and support.

How To Help Children With These Difficulties

All the principles in this book, centred on positive parenting and positive discipline, work with children with attention/activity problems; however, they may need to be applied more consistently and more patiently with these children. Whereas you might get away with an inconsistent routine with a normal child, a child with ADHD is likely to respond badly, with more difficult behaviour.

Whereas a normal child might easily sit down to homework for a long period of time in a relatively unstructured environment, a child with ADHD may need special support, lots of breaks and an environment free from distractions in order to complete the homework successfully.

Establish routines

Though all children benefit from predictable routines, this is especially the case with children with attention problems. Clear routines explained on a visual chart, with well defined and frequent breaks, can be really helpful in keeping children focused and managing with what is happening next. Also, active children can really benefit from including in the routine plenty of physical play and exercise (e.g. fifteen minutes of homework can be rewarded by some physical play or a walk – more likely a run!) See Step 5 for more information.

Take time to make sure your child understands what is expected

Children with attention problems can find it harder to process verbal instructions. Parents might have told the child several times to do something and the child appears not to have responded. This is often because the child is distracted and has not processed what the parent has said. Simple things like getting down to the child's level, making good eye contact, using very clear instructions and making sure the child has understood can make a real difference in helping them attend to what you are saying (see Step 6). Equally, reminders and warnings are also very helpful:

In another ten minutes, it is bedtime and you will have to tidy up.

When we are at the supermarket, you must stay by Mum's side.

Provide lots of encouragement and positive feedback

Because they are very active and impulsive, these children are often in trouble and tend to receive more negative feedback from parents and other adults (such as teachers). However, these children need encouragement just as much, and in some ways much more, than ordinary children. By consistently pointing out to them what they are doing right you build their confidence, but also help them learn how to behave well. The more specific you make your praise, the more you help them learn the skills they need:

Good boy, you finished that picture, well done.

You waited your turn, well done.

The difference with children with attention problems is that you have to work extra hard to make sure the encouragement goes through and that they understand the positive feedback you are giving. As with instructions, it helps to get down to the child's level, to use simple, clear language, to make sure they understand and to combine the praise with affection and other rewards. See Step 4 for more ideas on providing encouragement.

Problem solve

Usually their impulsivity is the main difficulty for these children (and the one that gets them into most trouble). As a result, the long-term aim is to help children learn to 'stop and think' before they act. Just as this book has been inviting parents to 'press the pause button' and choose different ways of acting, so you are hoping to help these children 'press the pause button' also and to learn better ways of resolving problems. You can do this in advance by discussing problems with children either if it comes up naturally in the conversation or by reading a special book with them, using examples that come up in everyday children's books about sharing. For example, when reading a story about a boy not sharing, you could say:

The boy in the story wants to play with his friend's train, but his friend won't let him. What could he do instead?

You can then help your child come up with lots of solutions and ideas for how to act, such as waiting to take a turn, asking nicely to play, going to play with something else etc. By thinking out solutions in advance, your children may remember to use them in the heat of the moment.

It can also help to problem-solve with children about an ongoing issue. Once again, the key is to help your child pause and think about the best way to act:

How can you stay sitting longer at your desk in class?

What can you do when you want something away from your desk?

Problem solving with children with attention difficulties takes a lot of time and patience, but it is worth it as it is the best long-term way of helping them learn to cope with their difficulties. See Step 9 for more information on problem solving with children.

Self-care for parents

Bringing up children who are over-active and impulsive is definitely hard work. While the principles described in this book can make a real difference and make things more manageable, they are not an overnight cure and mainly provide positive ways of coping. For this reason, parental self-care is very important. It is very hard to be consistent and positive twenty-four hours a day if your child is constantly demanding your attention, and it is very easy to get burnt out. For this reason you should prioritise breaks and relaxation for yourself, making sure to use babysitters and other supports to allow you to recharge and refuel.

The good news is that many of the problems that children with attention difficulties present with tend to fade over time as children mature and learn how to be less impulsive and more in control of their responses.

Seek assessment and support

Many parents find it useful to seek a formal assessment of their child's needs, which can lead to a range of extra supports. For children diagnosed with ADHD, several things can help:

- Special school support and programmes
- Extra consistent and positive parenting
- Educating people about the difficulty
- Medication.

One of the controversial treatments available to children diagnosed with ADHD is stimulant medication which has been shown to help some children accurately diagnosed regulate their impulsivity. Medication works best in the context of a wide range of interventions and supports and it should not be used in isolation. The best way to seek an assessment as to whether medication might benefit your child is via your local child mental health service, accessed through your GP.

Discipline Plan

Children who are overactive and impulsive can have associated behavioural problems and these can be dealt with in much the same positive way as used with other children (see steps on dealing with tantrums and oppositional behaviour). The principles behind Steps 6–8 apply equally well to these children. In particular, the focus on clear rules and giving children choices can be very effective once applied patiently and consistently. By giving children a chance to choose between keeping a rule and consequences, you invite them to pause and to consider how to respond, thus teaching them how to reduce their impulsivity.

Problem 5
Dealing with Abuse and Disrespect

My eight-year-old girl can speak so disrespectfully to me and her mother. You wouldn't believe the words that come out of her mouth when she gets into one of her outbursts. We all end up in a row, and really upset.

Most behaviour difficulties are not to do with *what a child is saying* but *how a child is saying it*. For example, if a child is upset at a rule such as not being allowed to go out, it is ok for them to tell you that they are upset or annoyed, but it is not ok for them to shout at you, swear at you or to become aggressive. It is the manner in which your child is talking to you that causes most of the problems.

Children communicate abusively to their parents for many different reasons. Sometimes it is because they have not learnt the skill of communicating positively; sometimes it is due to the fact that communicating disrespectfully gets them their way, as, at least some of the time, parents give in because of the abuse; sometimes it is because the 'uproar' the abuse causes is a reward (albeit a negative one). Whatever the reason, disrespectful communication is a habit that is usually reinforced by the parent's reaction (either anger or giving in), which is damaging to the parent–child relationship and which will cause social problems for the child if they do it outside the home. However, the good news is that with patience and hard work, the disrespect and abuse can be reduced and children can be taught how to communicate more respectfully.

The golden rule – At all times, your children must speak respectfully to you
One of the most important rules to insist upon with your children is that they must speak respectfully to you (even when upset and annoyed). As a parent, you deserve to be spoken to with politeness and courtesy.

The deal – At all times, as parent you must speak respectfully to your children

You must show your children how to communicate. You must role model for them how to talk respectfully and politely (even when you are feeling annoyed). How you behave towards your children is a much more powerful lesson than telling them what to do.

Discipline – Responding When Children Speak Abusively Or Disrespectfully To You

Address the disrespect, not the issue

One mistake that parents make when responding to a child being abusive is that they continue the argument or talk about the issue the child is raising rather than address the disrespectful way the child is speaking to them.

For example, a child may burst in the door, shouting abusively for her mother to find her runners. In response, the mother may get up and start searching for the runners, or she may get really angry in return and shout at the child about how careless she is, always leaving her stuff all over the house. Both reactions are unhelpful. In the first one, by getting up, the mother teaches the child that being abusive gets your mother to do what you want. In the second, by being abusive in return the mother exacerbates the row and models a disrespectful way of communication. Neither reaction addresses the disrespect nor shows the child how to communicate properly.

Instead, a better response is for the parent to first address how the child is communicating, before dealing with the issue of the runners. For example, the parent could say:

> *Julie, you are shouting now, I can only listen when you speak politely.*

> *Julie, I appreciate you are in a hurry, but I can only help you when you ask politely.*

Then the parent should wait until the child rephrases her request politely before she responds to the issue (of the missing runners). This 'first address the disrespect' principle applies in other situations when the parent is making a request of the child. For example, suppose a parent is trying to have a serious conversation with their child about staying out late and the child is being disrespectful by being sarcastic or turning their back and refusing to listen. In this instance, the parent shouldn't continue the conversation about the issue (of staying out late) but should instead address the way the child is communicating, saying something like:

John, turn round and listen, this is important.

John, if you don't turn around and listen, then you won't be able to go out at all tomorrow.

Show your child the tone of voice you want

Disrespect is usually communicated by tone of voice. Sarcasm, anger and contempt are all implied through different tones of voice. When a child speaks in a disrespectful tone the temptation is to mirror that tone back to them. For example, when a child shouts at you, it is very easy to shout back. However, in order to teach a child about respectful communication, it is very important that you always use a respectful tone back to the child. So even if your child shouts, you return a calm (albeit firm and assertive) tone of voice. This has the affect of helping the child calm down and de-escalating the situation and also models to the child a better way of communicating.

It can also be helpful to take this a step further and to explicitly point out the tone you want the child to use. For example, when the child was shouting at the mother to find her runners, the parent might respond:

Listen Julie, I can only listen to you when you ask me politely.

Julie, if you were to say something like, 'Mum, where are my runners?' in a pleasant tone of voice, then I would be able to help.

Some children need this level of guidance in speaking politely and respectfully.

Step-by-step action plan – shouting and abuse

Many parents find it helpful to have a step-by-step action plan in order to deal with challenging behaviour (see Step 7). When dealing with abuse, sometimes a child can respond angrily when you start addressing the disrespect and it can be helpful to think through all the 'What Ifs' – how you will respond to whatever reaction your child has. Consider the possible step-by-step plan below:

1. If my child shouts at me I will respond calmly and assertively, saying:

    John, I can only talk to you when you speak calmly.

2. If my child continues to shout, then I will pull back and not argue with him. I won't discuss the issue while he is shouting.

3. If my child continues to shout or the row escalates, I will give him a choice:

    John, if you continue to shout you will lose some pocket money
    and then I will pull back calmly.

4. If my child continues to shout, I will remain calm and get on with things around the house, showing my child that I am calm and not letting his anger affect me.

5. If I do speak to him while he is shouting, I will remind him gently to calm down:

    C'mon John, if you calm down now you won't lose any more pocket money.

Prevention Plan – Teaching A Child Respectful Communication

The discipline plan above is also prevention, in that by dealing with a child's disrespect in a respectful way you model to the child the proper way to communicate – and children always learn more from what we *show* them than what we *tell* them.

There are also other things you can do to teach respectful communication and reduce the likelihood of disrespectful outbursts:

Keep providing positive attention

Because abuse is so personally wounding, it is easy for parents to build up resentment and to reduce the amount of positive attention their children receive at other times. However, to help your children change, you need to keep the positive channels open to them. It is important not to dwell on past incidents, to move on (once you deal with them assertively this is much easier) and to continue all the other positive aspects of parenting such as play/special time, listening, praise and encouragement (at other times) etc. These maintain your connection with your child and make change possible (see Steps 2, 3 and 4).

Problem solving

Sometimes it is useful to talk through the problem of shouting or tantrums with your children (Step 9). The purpose can be to help them articulate their feelings and frustrations in positive ways that don't involve disrespecting anyone. Some children are open to discussing what makes them lose their temper and to exploring strategies for remaining calm in difficult situations (these are good conversations for parents and children alike). For example, you can brainstorm with your children about ways they can 'press the pause button' in the heat of the moment, and they might suggest that they pull back and not say anything disrespectful. Many of the ideas that can be identified include:

- Taking a slow, deep breath
- Counting to ten (or distracting oneself with something else)
- Taking a break and pulling back
- Saying something positive and calming ('I am going to remain calm').

The key to problem solving with children is not to use the time to tell your children off for misbehaving, but to instead explore new, more positive ways of behaving:

Parent: Listen, John, it is not ok to shout at someone like that.

John: I don't mean to … I just get so annoyed.

Parent: It is ok to be angry and to say you are upset, but it is not ok to be rude or to speak rudely …

John: (pause)

Parent: Well, how can you stop being disrespectful? How can you calm yourself when you get annoyed?

John: Dunno.

Parent: Well, let's think, what could you do when you feel yourself getting annoyed?

John: I could walk away …

Parent: Yes, walk away, that is a good idea. Let's think of other ones.

A good opportunity to problem solve is when the child apologises after being abusive or after a tantrum:

Parent: I appreciate that you are sorry, but you need to do more than that. You need to make sure not to speak like that again.

John: (shrugs)

Parent: So what can you do to ensure you don't speak like that again?

John: Dunno.

Parent: Well, let's think about it …

Address underlying issues

In some instances, children being abusive can be understood in the context of other issues within the family. Some children feel excluded in the family, or jealous of other siblings, or feel inadequate in school because they are finding it a struggle or even because they are being bullied. While these do not excuse the disrespect, it can help to take steps to deal with the specific underlying problems (see problems regarding sibling rivalry and homework).

Further reading

Warwick Dyer, *Mercury's Child – Behaviour Change System*, www. behaviourchange.com.

Problem 6
Severe Tantrums

My seven-year-old boy throws really big tantrums when he does not get his own way. They can last for hours. He often becomes really threatening towards me and he wears me down. Sometimes I am reduced to tears. I feel we are walking on eggshells in the house, trying not to upset him or provoke another tantrum.

Perhaps the hardest behaviour problem to deal with is persistent and extended tantrums. Though these can be normal enough with a young child of two, they become harder to deal with as the child gets older, with the possibility of the behaviour becoming a fixed pattern. Some parents experience long tantrums involving a child badgering them or being abusive and disrespectful, or shouting and screaming for several hours, or even the whole day, to get them to change a discipline decision or as a means of expressing their upset. Many parents describe 'walking on eggshells' with some children, whereby they fear provoking the child and a tantrum and do everything to avoid this. When it has come to this stage, you have surrendered your control to your child and you are letting your child be in charge by their use of negative tactics. This is not helpful to either you or your child.

The key to dealing with tantrums is to think through a plan of action that allows you to remain calm and positive and which you are confident that you can carry out, even in the most challenging situations. By having a plan of action, you regain control and you make decisions based on the rules and what is right rather than what your child wants. Dealing with tantrums is very similar to dealing with abuse and disrespect, as covered in Problem 5. Below are some other principles to bear in mind.

Dealing With Tantrums Calmly And Positively

Press the pause button

The key is to not argue or get hooked into your child's tantrum. Pull back and don't give your child too much attention. Instead, think of what might be the best way to respond – make sure you remain in control. When dealing with a tantrum, essentially you have a choice:

a.   If you give in to the child and give them their demand, you may stop the current tantrum, *but you increase the number of future tantrums as the child learns to use tantrums as a means of getting their own way*

or

b.   You sit out the tantrum calmly and positively without giving in. The current tantrum may last longer, *but there will be less frequent ones in the future as the child learns that tantrums do not get them their own way.*

Get on with ordinary business

If you can, don't put everything on hold while your child is 'tantruming', as this gives the child control. Instead, try and go about doing what you would have being doing had there been no tantrum. This gives the child the message that life goes on, that their negative behaviour does not control you and that this is not the way to influence people. This actually can make a young child feel safe – that it is their parents and not them who are in control.

Keep talk to a minimum

Talk minimally to your child while they are in a tantrum, and when you do:

- Make sure your tone remains polite, firm and positive
- Don't get into an argument about the issue (e.g. lecture him on why the rule was necessary)
- State what you want to happen – 'John, come on, let's calm down and we can talk'.

Enforce consequences for each part of the tantrum as necessary

Essential to dealing with ongoing tantrums is the setting up of a clear discipline system consisting of consequences and sanctions with your children (see Steps 6–8). You can use these sanctions for each part of the tantrum that is causing problems:

John, for each minute you go on shouting, you will lose 10 cent of your pocket money.

John, if you throw things on the floor you will only have to tidy them up later.

Come on John, I don't want you to lose any more money; if you calm down now, you won't lose any more.

As with all discipline, the key is to offer these consequences as a choice to the child and to deliver them in a calm, respectful (rather than a provocative) way. See Steps 7 and 8 for more details.

Don't take behaviour personally

Though this can be very hard in the heat of the moment, it helps not to take your child's behaviour personally, but to see it as a sign that your child just hasn't yet learnt the skill of managing their angry feelings; by being positive, calm and respectful and by using consequences you will teach them how to manage their anger and to behave more responsibly.

Sometimes soothing helps
Sometimes it helps to soothe and coach a child to calm down:

Look John, I know you are upset about not being able to go out, but it is important that you calm down.

John, it's ok to be upset at not going out, but it is not ok to shout or be rude.

Timing is very important with soothing and it works best when a child has become quite upset and needs some help calming down. If, when you try to soothe, your child tries again to draw you into an argument, then it is best to pull back.

Sometimes distraction can help
Sometimes it can help to focus your child on something else, for example saying:

John, dinner will be ready soon; shall we set the table?

This can help a child get back into behaving well. Though like soothing, the timing of offering a distraction is crucial, and this is best near the end of a tantrum when the child needs some 'way out' signalled to him.

Practice relaxation and deep breathing
The key to getting through a tantrum is not letting it get to you and remaining calm and positive. This is hard! Practicing deep breathing or positive thinking can help.

Establish a step-by-step plan
In difficult situations, it can help to think through a step-by-step plan for how you will respond to the different behaviours that your child might exhibit during a tantrum. As it is hard to think in the heat of the moment, this can help ensure you respond calmly and positively. For example:

- **If my child badgers me**, I will say, 'John, keep your distance please'.
- **If my child follows me**, I will get up and leave the room and go about my business.
- **If my child gets aggressive**, I will assertively say, 'John, keep your

hands to yourself' and pull away (I may impose another consequence later for this).

The key is that you pause and think about how best to respond. All the methods above can work once you are in charge and not reacting. 'Tune into' yourself and your child and this will give you a sense of what will work, but it is important to be patient and persistent.

Prevention Plan – Teaching Your Child To Communicate Without Resorting To Tantrums

Children who have got into a pattern of using tantrums to communicate are usually unhappy children often suffering from a lack of confidence and acutely aware of everyone's resentful feelings towards them for behaving badly (though at the same time unsure as to how to change). In addition to a discipline plan to help them change, these children need all the positive aspects of parenting and for their parents to maintain a positive connection with them. Thus, to balance an effective discipline plan like the one above, it is important to also have a prevention plan to maintain a positive relationship with your child and to teach them how to communicate positively, without resorting to tantrums.

The principle for this prevention plan is identical to the one covered in the last chapter on dealing with abuse and disrespect (see Problem 5 for details).

Problem 7
Anxious, Worried Children

My seven-year-old daughter can be very anxious when meeting new people. She becomes really shy and just closes down. This is not like the talkative girl I know at home.

My ten-year-old son is a constant worrier. He can work himself up about something small such as an issue in school and then he will be thinking about it all day, worrying.

My six year old is really afraid of dogs. If he thinks one is nearby he can become really frightened and plans his life around avoiding any contact.

Anxiety and fears are part and parcel of childhood and most children go through phases of having certain fears or being anxious about certain events and situations. Many children, however, experience excessive over-anxiety and need special support and help from their parents and others in coping, and this is what we will look at now.

What children feel anxious about

What anxieties and fears affect children often depends on their age and their personality. For example, it is perfectly normal for an eighteen-month-old child to become anxious when separated from their mother or for a four year old to be fearful of dogs or for a six year old to have occasional nightmares or for a nine year old to be anxious about fitting in with new friends. Anxieties are usually categorised as follows:

Separation anxiety. Toddlers usually experience anxiety when they are separated from their parents; for example, when they are left with babysitters or at a crèche. For most children this is temporary and they can quickly settle. School children can also feel separation anxiety at times, whether this is when they are going to school or staying away from home for a night or visiting relatives. In extreme cases it can lead to a child refusing to go to school or to be apart from their parents.

Phobias. Children can also develop specific fears focused on certain situations or things, such as being scared of dogs or the dark. Usually the child is fearful of something specific happening, whether this is being bitten by the dog, or there being a 'monster' in the dark. A phobia could be caused by a specific event (such as being chased by a dog) but in many situations there is no specific cause.

Social fears or shyness. It is normal for many children to be shy in company or to take some time before they warm up and get to know other children. For some children this fear can be quite pronounced as they worry excessively about new social situations and may avoid making new friends.

Specific worries. Many children can worry about bad events or disasters happening, such as the car crashing or the house going on fire or their parents dying from an illness. This is often provoked by seeing news items about these things happening or watching movies which increase these fears.

Nightmares. Nightmares are very common in children between the ages of two and eight. While nightmares can happen more frequently after a traumatic event, in most cases there is no specific cause and they are generally thought to be the result of the everyday worries and stresses associated with growing up.

What You Can Do To Help Your Child

Support and reassure your child

The most important thing you can do when faced by your children's anxiety is to be there to listen and support them. Help them open up and talk about what is worrying them and acknowledge their feelings and fears. Children feel great relief when someone has heard and understood what is worrying them. While hearing children's worries can be upsetting, it is much better that they are sharing them with you and not bottling them up and dealing with them alone.

Be Aware Of Your Own Feelings And Worries

Many parents find it hard to listen to their children's worries because it brings up their own worries or they are troubled that their child feels this way. Try and respond calmly when your children express a worry. The more you can be confident and reassuring, the more you will help them cope.

Problem solve with your child

Once a worry has been identified, a good response is to problem solve with your child about ways to address what is worrying them (see Step 9). As well as coming up with ideas or taking action yourself, it is useful to encourage your child to think up solutions and to take part in sorting out what is worrying them. For example:

- If your daughter is feeling shy or anxious about a new social situation, you could explore with her how she might approach and talk to the other children, who she might play with and what games she might play.

- If your son is worried about getting a school project finished, you might explore with him what he has already done, what he needs to do for the next step and how he could structure his work.

- If your son has a particular fear about dogs, you might reassure him about how you will protect him and also discuss how he can keep away from dogs that worry him. You may also discuss how he could approach a safe, child-friendly dog with your support – but only at his pace.

There are many situations where it is important for parents to take action to protect their children. For example, if your child talks of being bullied or excluded in school, it is appropriate to take action by contacting the school teacher. However, it is usually best to first discuss with your children what action you are going to take and to encourage them to take action also (especially with older children).

Coping with worries

For many of the worries that children raise, there are no specific or immediate solutions. For example, a lot of children worry about something bad happening, such as a car crash or a fire or even their parents dying. Often these worries are associated with children having witnessed or being through a similar event in the past. In those instances, while supporting these children through these worries can be hard, there are a lot of things that can help.

Listen carefully and empathise

In a desire to help, many parents either dismiss or over-reassure a child when they express a worry, which can mean that the child does not get space to express it. It is always useful to listen carefully to what children are worried about and to help them express what they are feeling. The key is to express empathy and help them feel understood:

> *It is understandable that you feel fearful about car crashes when you hear about them on the news.*

> *When someone special dies, many children feel worried about other people dying.*

Once you have heard what your child is worried about and communicated a sense that you understand, then you are in a position to reassure and support them and they are more likely to hear your reassurance:

> *Of course, it is very unlikely that we will crash, and we will always drive safely.*

> *Mum and Dad are very healthy at the moment; we plan to be around for a long time.*

Express belief that your child will cope

Many children who are prone to anxiety generate lots of 'what ifs' about all the bad things that could happen. While it is useful to reassure them and answer some of their concerns, be wary of trying to answer every 'what if' about your children's worries as this is impossible. Most important is that you communicate a belief to your children that, whatever happens, you believe they will cope and work it out and that you will be there to support them.

Help your child come up with coping strategies
A lot of children who are prone to anxiety can benefit from learning coping strategies to deal with their anxiety. These can include helping children to learn:

- Relaxation techniques such as deep breathing that can deal with all worries
- Positive visualisation such as imagining a happy place or repeating a positive affirmation when a worry is bothering them
- Distracting them with fun activities, such as exercise, playing etc.

Focus on things other than the worries
Whatever your child is worried about, it is important not to let the worry become central or to take over their lives. As well as listening and coming up with strategies, it is important to communicate the message that life goes on and to focus on other enjoyable things. This simply means ensuring that the everyday routine of homework, school, play, fun times, family time goes on as normal.

Dealing with over-worrying
If your child brings up continual worries, a useful strategy is to set aside a regular worry time. This means agreeing with your child that you will set aside a special worry time (such as fifteen minutes just after school) when you will listen carefully to all her worries and help her sort them out, but for the rest of the day you agree to only talk about other happy things. If she brings up a worry, respond with something like, 'We'll talk about that later' and then distract her with something else. With continual worriers, plan to

do lots of 'worry-free' and happy activities which can build their confidence and which you can both enjoy.

Seek support

If you feel anxiety or worry is interfering with your child getting on with their life, then do consider getting special support and help. The good news is that children with anxiety problems often benefit from counselling and special support. They tend to be quite self-aware about the problem and motivated to get help – qualities which can make counselling successful. Counselling generally focuses on many of the strategies we have discussed above:

- Helping children express their anxieties and feel understood
- Problem solving any issues
- Teaching coping strategies (relaxation, positive thinking, distraction etc.)

Sources of support can include your local child mental health service (via your GP), or school-based counselling.

Build your child's confidence in the long term

Anxiety is often associated with poor confidence or low self-esteem so it can be very helpful to build your child's self-esteem and confidence. This can include:

- Setting aside daily play and fun times
- Creating positive family rituals
- Helping your child get involved in projects they can enjoy and succeed in
- Helping your child make supportive and good friends.

See the next two chapters (Problems 8 and 9) on friendship and self-esteem for more details.

Problem 8
Trouble with Making Friends

My eight-year-old son is an only child and seems to be having trouble making friends. He can be really competitive when playing with children his own age and this can set them against him. This is especially the case in football or other team games where he often ends up isolated.

Being able to make friends is a very important part of childhood, especially as your child enters primary school, where forming friendships is key to their self-esteem and their learning important social skills. Studies have shown that children who are able to form close friendships in childhood are more likely to succeed later on in school and less likely to be lonely as young adults. However, forming friendships can be far from easy and some children can have special difficulties in this area. The good news is that there are lots of constructive things that parents can do to help.

Why Children Have Difficulty Making Friends

There are many different reasons as to why some children find it hard to make and keep friends. Some children find it harder to learn the social skills that are necessary to make friendships, whether this is how to join in games, how to share or how to listen. Some children have other behavioural difficulties such as oppositional behaviour, or attention difficulties which can make it harder to keep good friends (see related problems). Some children may have autistic-type difficulties such as Asperger's syndrome, a key feature of which is social skills difficulties. These children will benefit from special assessment and support and child mental health and disability services.

However, many children find it hard to make friends simply because they have not had the opportunity. We live in a world where children's lives are full of passive entertainments such as TV, computers, PlayStations etc., which can often result in children having little time to socially interact with other children. Even children with busy schedules of sports and learning activities may not have the necessary 'down time' to hang out and spend time with friends.

Supporting Children In Making And Keeping Friends

Help your child meet friends

Often the difficulty for children is simply meeting other children who could become friends. They may go to school out of the area or live in a neighbourhood where there are few children their age. Or they could come into contact with lots of children, but they don't share their interests, or they have never got over the hurdle of getting a friendship started. There are lots of things that you can do to help.

Take an interest in your child's activities and potential friendships

Ask your children about who they meet at school or at other activities. Crucially, ask about which children they like or get on with or share an interest with and who they might like to invite over to play. Some children who have trouble making friends often aren't forthcoming with their parents about who they meet and what they do at school or other events. In these situations, parents often have to be more proactive, and this can mean spending more time at your child's activities, whether this is lingering after a scouts meeting or watching your child in the school yard to see who they talk to and get on with; in this way you can ask them more about it later e.g. 'Who was the boy you were playing ball with? He seems nice?' At other times you can ask about the children your child seems close to and ask whether they would like to invite them over to play.

Encourage social activities that promote friendships

Aside from school, one of most common places children meet potential new friends is in organised activities in the local area such as sports, scouts, clubs and special interests etc. However, the key to making this work is to pick the activity carefully. It should be an activity that is well supervised by an adult, that your child enjoys, is already good at, knows the rules, and which allows for social time. (This means not pushing your child into a new sport that you feel they should be good at – especially if your focus is on encouraging friendships.)

Of course, some children will resist starting any new activities – especially if they have had bad experiences in the past of feeling rejected etc. In these situations it can be a case of searching with them for an activity they really like, doing a lot of preparation to ensure they are ready for the activity and striking a deal that they have to only attend two or three times and then they can decide themselves if they want to continue.

It is important to only schedule one special activity at a time. Many children are over-scheduled and bombarded with too much input. One good activity attended well is far better than several rushed to and attended poorly.

Get to know parents of potential friends for your children

If your child has difficulty meeting new friends, it can be a good idea to create opportunities for them to meet new children. This can be as simple as making an effort to get to know neighbours who have children of a similar age or who might share your child's interests. The key to making this work is to follow your child's lead. For example, it is understandable to introduce your child to children who are convenient for you to meet, such as children of friends, relations etc. While these groups are often great sources of potential friends, this will not always be the case – and you need to check carefully as to whether the children genuinely like each other or have things in common (and are not just brought together for the convenience of their parents).

Set up play dates for your child

One of the most important things you can do to support your children making and keeping friends is to arrange regular play dates for them with another child. The key to making a play date work is that it:

- Has the agreement and support of both sets of parents
- Should involve a friend that your child wants to play with and with whom they have a lot in common (as opposed to one that is convenient for you!)
- Is ideally one to one (as this is the best way for your child to make a close friend), which means that you can't expect older or younger siblings to join in – your child should be given sufficient space
- Is supervised by an adult: though the children are given space to play, a parent is supportively there and available in the background
- Involves interactive toys and games: TV viewing and overuse of computer games should be banned from the play date and your child should be encouraged to think of better alternatives.

It is also important to plan the play date with your child and talk about it once it is finished – asking about what they played etc. and making sure to encourage any good play skills.

Encourage your child's friendship skills

The skills of making friendships do not come easily to some, and many children can exhibit behaviours (e.g. being competitive or negative) that make it harder for them to make and keep friends. However, you can do a lot to help your children learn these skills.

Go over skills

Sometimes simply going over the skills with children or coaching your child prior to starting a new activity can be really helpful. For example, you can ask your son to remind you of all the important skills of 'being a good team player' or 'playing like a friend' and list them with him:

- Waiting your turn
- Praising other children
- Sharing
- Playing your best
- Keeping the rules.

Read books together
There are many good child-centred story books and TV programmes that emphasise good friendship skills. Introduce these as part of your night-time reading with your child. Take time to discuss the ideas in each story with your child and to review what they have learnt.

Model social skills in your own play with your children
Probably your child will learn most from how you play with them. So if you model turn-taking, praise, sharing, playing your best, keeping the rules when you play with your child on a one-to-one basis, this will help them learn to do this also.

Join your child in play with a friend
Sometimes it can be helpful to join your child for a period of time as they play with a friend or another child in order to model some good play skills and to directly encourage any you see in the game. For example, this can be as simple as making comments such as:

John, you are waiting your turn – good lad.

Julie, that was nice that you shared your doll with Alice.

Peter, that was a nice thing to say to Paul.

Problem solve with your child about friendships
All the skills of problem solving (Step 9) are very important in supporting your child in making friendships and in sorting out any problems that may arise. This can be done in advance by anticipating

potential problems as they come up in conversation (or in general when you are reading or watching TV together). You can ask your child good questions such as:

How come all the team were angry at the boy in the film?

What could he have done to become a good team player?

You can use problem solving to tackle any worries or concerns your child has about friendships. For example, if your daughter is wondering about how to fit in in the school yard, you could ask:

Parent:	How could you join in with a group of girls when they are playing?
Jane:	I could just ask them could I play?
Parent:	Yes, that is a good idea … but even before that, what should you do?
Jane:	I could wait and see what they are playing and see if I want to play it.
Parent:	Yes … watching first is always a good idea.

Problem solving can be used in most situations. For a child who is nervous about asking a friend over, you could explore with them what the best way is to ask them, and you could even rehearse the telephone call with them. Or for a child who has gotten into a row with a friend, you could discuss with them how they can make up and what might be the best way to apologise, if appropriate.

Further reading

Fred Frankel, *Good Friends are Hard to Find: Help your child find, make and keep friends*, Los Angeles, Perspective Publishing, 1996.

Problem 9

Children with Low Self-Esteem or Poor Confidence

My ten year old really lacks confidence. She worries about getting things right, can be a bit of a perfectionist and is very sensitive to being put down. Last week when I spoke to her about something minor she got really upset, saying she 'couldn't do anything right'. I am really worried that her lack of confidence will affect her as she grows up. What can I do to build her self-esteem?

Having low self-esteem means thinking the worst about yourself, putting yourself down or suffering a lack of confidence in certain situations. Many children suffer from low self-esteem and this is often a worry for parents who are concerned that their children will be handicapped as they grow older because of it. While there are no overnight solutions, there is a lot you can do to boost your child's self-esteem and to help them develop more confidence and a better self-image. Positive parenting and good experiences at home can make a real difference.

What Causes Low Self-Esteem?

Low self-esteem in children has many different causes and origins and there is no specific agreement among experts. Many children have a sensitive or perfectionist personality that makes them more sensitive to criticism or more likely to be self-critical. Sometimes it is to do with the child having negative experiences, whether this is struggling in school, not fitting in or being excluded by friends, or being over-criticised or feeling put down within the family.

The sources of a child's self-esteem or how they feel about themselves is different at different ages. For example, during the pre-school years, experiences within the family are paramount; once a child starts school, experiences outside the home become much more significant. As the child approaches adolescence, peer influences become very powerful and a child's self-esteem is strongly affected by what messages they are receiving from the peer group they meet regularly.

It is important to remember that a child's confidence or self-esteem is not a fixed entity. It changes in different situations. For example, a child could feel very insecure and unconfident at school where he is struggling, yet the reverse when involved in a hobby that he enjoys and where he meets good friends. Equally, individual children are very different – one child may cope very well with a bad experience and another may take it to heart so that it becomes damaging to their self-esteem.

Address Any Problems That Are Affecting Your Child's Self-Esteem

If your child's confidence has changed recently – for example if you notice that your child is struggling in school or not accepted by a peer group or not making friends – take action to deal with this. This might mean meeting with the school to discuss getting special help for your child or helping them find new friends or peer groups. If you feel your child is being bullied, schools should have very clear policies on dealing with this and they should take your concerns seriously. Do whatever you can so your child can return to having positive learning and social experiences.

Boosting Children's Self-Esteem In The Long Term

Building children's confidence and self-esteem is a long-term project and a parent's role is crucial – there are many positive parenting habits that can help (see Steps 2–4 in Part 1 in particular):

1. Be very encouraging towards your child
Frequent, clear, genuine and specific praise is the best way to build a

child's confidence. Children should receive many more praise statements from their parents than criticisms (some people recommend four praises to every single criticism). The trick to making praise work is to be very specific and personal. Rather than saying 'Good boy' or 'Good girl', it is more effective to say, 'Thanks for tidying your toys up, it means a lot to me'.

2. Listen to your child

Listening is one of the most important parenting skills. Having your feelings acknowledged, your ideas valued and your experience heard is the biggest boost to self-esteem and self-worth. Make sure you have a daily 'listening time' with your children, where they can tell you their news and whatever is going on in their lives. Many parents find just after school, mealtimes, or just before bed good times to check in and listen to their children.

3. Model positive self-esteem

Children are more affected by what parents do than by what parents say. If you constantly put yourself down or are very self-critical in front of children, then this is the role model they learn. Conversely, if you show good self-esteem, then you give them a positive role model to follow. Having good self-esteem as a parent means being able to self-praise and encourage in front of children (saying something like 'I feel pleased about how I handled that') and being balanced and honest when you make a mistake ('I am sorry about what happened, I will do it differently the next time').

4. Remind your children of your love for them

Saying 'I love you' to your children or demonstrating your love for them on a regular basis is crucial to helping children feel deeply loved and cared for by you. Expressing your belief in your children and that you love them no matter what are all important messages to get through to them.

5. Create positive family rituals

Teach your children the habit of being grateful and affirming what is good in their life. In religious families this can be teaching children to say nightly prayers, when they thank God for the good things in their life and express love for all the people close to them.

6. Help your child get involved in projects in which they can be successful

Recognising your child's talents and interests and giving them an opportunity to succeed at these will really boost a child's self-esteem. If your child is good at a sport or crosswords or baking or whatever, make sure they can complete these tasks from beginning to end. This is particularly important for children who feel unsuccessful or feel that they 'get nothing right' – take time with this child to find something they enjoy and can succeed at with your support and encouragement.

7. Help your child make supportive and good friends

Good friendships are crucial to good self-esteem. Remember, each child's needs are different. For example, while one child may fit in with a 'sporty' group of friends, another may be more at home with friends from the computer or chess club. Help your child find a peer group that is good for them (see also the points on friendships in Problem 8).

A Final Thought

Remember, bringing up a happy, confident and well-adjusted child is a long-term project. There are no magic fixes to self-esteem problems, and what is required is loving, gentle, patient and persistent parenting.

Problem 10
Fussy Eating/Mealtime Battles

My six year old simply won't eat any vegetables. He refuses most of the healthy foods I give him. Even if I hide them in other food, he will pick them out one by one. He would live on chicken nuggets if I let him.

Mealtimes can be such a battle with our seven-year-old daughter. She won't stay at the table or eat all her food. I am worried that she is not getting enough nutrients.

One of the most stressful things about parenting can be trying to feed nutritious food to a resistant young child. Feeding is the primary task of being a parent, and as a result it can be such an emotive issue. As a parent, you can easily worry about whether your child is getting enough nutrition or you can feel a failure if your child won't eat what you have prepared. It is easy to take as personal your child's refusal to eat – it is hard to accept your child rejecting the food that you have spent so much time, care and love preparing. As a result, mealtimes can become a source of conflict or a 'battle of wills' to get your child to eat. Such battles are only counter-productive as they focus a lot of negative attention on 'not eating' as opposed to positive attention on eating well.

In addition, children can have very different styles of eating. Some children can keep to a routine of three meals a day, but others tend to have a more 'grazing' style of eating, whereby they eat smaller amounts but more frequently throughout the day (leading to them eating roughly the same amount as other children). One way to help these children is to ensure you have more regular meals and lots of healthy snacks.

Dealing with fussy eating or mealtime battles requires both a prevention plan to foster healthy eating habits and also a discipline plan to reduce conflict during mealtimes.

Prevention – Fostering Healthy Eating Habits In Young Children

Be a great role model

In the long term, children are most likely to learn from how you behave rather than what you tell them. The more you can be a role model to your children about eating healthy food, the better. If your children see you eating *and enjoying* vegetables and other healthy foods, this will most likely influence them. If your children see you grabbing an apple as a snack (and once again enjoying it!) they will be tempted to try one. If, on the other hand, they get the message that vegetables don't taste nice and are instead merely to be 'endured' before dessert, they are likely to follow suit.

Expose your child to healthy food

Aside from parents being good role models, research shows that repeated exposure and experience of healthy food and vegetables is the best way to get children to eat them. This means you make sure to have a range of vegetables available at meals and a bowl of fruit on the table (which you encourage as the first port of call for a snack). There are other creative ways to expose children to vegetables and healthy food such as:

- Involving children in the preparation of the food. Show them how to cut and chop vegetables or how to make a nutritious smoothie or how to cook a healthy stew
- Setting up a vegetable plot in the garden and getting your child to help with planting the seeds and harvesting the results
- Involving your child in shopping for food and in choosing which vegetables to have for dinner.

Make mealtimes relaxed, enjoyable times

Try and make mealtimes a relaxed, enjoyable experience and try to remove any pressure to eat from mealtimes. Food is most enjoyed when it can be eaten slowly. Make sure you are not rushing but have time to sit with your child as they eat. Research shows that children are more likely to settle at the table to eat when their parents are sitting with them eating at the same time (rather than rushing around to serve or standing up eating themselves). Aside from encouraging healthy eating, the routine of a relaxed family meal has many other benefits for children and parents, such as giving them time to chat and connect with one another.

Make sure to offer your child small portions

Parents often overestimate what their child needs to eat. It is better to start with small portions of food and encourage your child to ask for more if needed. Young children are often more adapted to eating 'little and often' rather than three square meals a day. If this is the case, you are likely to be more successful in having smaller but more frequent meals. Where possible, try and give your children choices about their food (as this encourages them to take responsibility for what they eat). For example, maybe have two vegetables in the centre of the table and invite them to choose which one they want to eat first.

Be creative about how you introduce vegetables and healthy food

The trick to helping your children eat healthy food is to keep introducing it and offering it to them, even if they initially appear uninterested. Try lots of different ways of presenting food. For example, carrots can be eaten raw or cooked, served in a soup or added to a smoothie. They can also be 'hidden' in mashed potato or in a meatloaf. You could also make your child's favourite dip (such as guacamole) and then cut the carrots into batons for them to eat with it. Sometimes, simply presenting vegetables in a different container can make a difference – the carrots might appear more appealing in a favourite cup or beaker.

When you introduce a new food to a child, make sure to introduce it with familiar ones they like. Also, be patient about how much they will try (maybe only a mouthful the first time).

Encourage discipline about snacks and sweets

While it is generally not recommended to bribe or pressure children to eat healthy foods – 'you won't get any sweets until you eat your carrots' – (as this can give a message that vegetables aren't enjoyable), it is a good idea to encourage discipline about sweets and snacks. It is good to help children get into the habit of eating their dinner first before their dessert.

Be patient

Fostering healthy eating habits is a long-term job and it is important to be patient. Remember, children's appetites and tastes are changing all the time; even if they don't like a food now, this may change when you introduce it again in the future, perhaps in a new, novel way.

Discipline – When A Child Is Refusing To Eat

Pause – unhook from a battle of wills

The first step is to pause and unhook from a battle of wills. Trying to pressurise a child to eat is a battle you will always lose. Instead, it can be useful to pull back for a minute and to concentrate on something else – perhaps eating your own food or distracting your child by talking about something else or attending to other children at the table. This pause gives you a chance to think about how to respond.

Ignore poor eating; attend when your child eats instead

It is very easy to get hooked into mainly attending when your child is not eating (e.g. focusing on how much food is left or the fact that they have not tried any vegetables). This can build resistance and negativity. Another tactic is to instead go out of your way to attend to and encourage your child any time they *do* eat. Often this is about making simple comments such as:

You are trying some of the potato – good boy.

You like the nuggets – they are tasty.

Look! You have already eaten half your vegetables.

You can also use your positive attention to help your child eat by attending to and noticing other children at the table who are eating:

Pete, you have finished all your peas; would you like some more?

Give choices
Offering your child choices is a good way of encouraging them to take responsibility for eating. This can be as simple as inviting:

Which vegetable would you like to eat today?

You can have carrots or peas today – which would you like?

When you eat your dinner, you will be able to have some dessert.

Let children experience consequences for not eating
You can help your children experience natural consequences for not eating by setting up a fixed routine for mealtimes (see Step 7). For example:

- The time for dinner is set for a fixed period e.g. from 5pm to 5:30pm

- The new routine is explained in advance to the children

- If your child has not eaten their food by 5:25pm, you give a warning that they have five more minutes to finish

- At 5:30pm you calmly put away all the food, and only have more food available at the next mealtime

- If your child asks for food in between meals, you calmly and positively say, 'Well, supper will be at 7pm and you can have some nice food then'.

The key to making this discipline work is to not provide any unhealthy snacks between mealtimes and to calmly stick to your rule. For example, if your child comes to you complaining that they are hungry, you resist the temptation to lecture – 'Well, why didn't you eat your dinner?' – (increasing the battle), or to give in and give a snack to your child (reinforcing bad eating habits), and instead calmly remind them of the next mealtime. The idea is that children will learn from being a little hungry to make sure to eat the healthy food during the mealtimes. By calmly enforcing the discipline in this way, all the 'battle' is taken out of mealtimes.

Some parents who worry about children getting enough nutrients often find this discipline hard to implement. An alternative in these situations is to make a healthy snack available, such as a piece of fruit, if a child is hungry between meals. In this way you are reassured that your child is eating healthily and isn't going hungry.

Problem 11
Telling Lies

My seven-year-old girl is starting to lie a lot. She will make up stories for no reason. The other day she told me that she got star pupil of the week. When I asked the teacher about it, she said it wasn't true. When I tell her off, or ask her why she told a lie, she closes down and doesn't say anything.

My nine-year-old son often tells lies. Last week, one of the vases in the house was broken. I know it was him, as he was the only one in the house at the time, but he absolutely swears it wasn't. It hurts me that he won't tell the truth.

Children telling lies can be quite hurtful or embarrassing to parents, especially if you (as most parents do) place a high value on honesty. Though all children tell lies from time to time, it is easy to take your children's lies personally or as a slight on your values. Children tell lies for many different reasons and it is first important to understand why. Telling lies can be used to:

* Avoid getting into trouble ('I didn't break the glass')
* Gain a treat ('Daddy said we could have a piece of cake')
* Get out of something unpleasant ('The teacher did not give us any homework today')
* Gain attention or approval ('I won the star in school today').

Sometimes lying is infrequent and once off and sometimes it becomes part of an ongoing pattern or habit. In these situations it is important to take action and to think of ways of teaching your child to tell the truth.

Discipline – Responding When Your Child Tells A Lie

Press the pause button

As in many discipline situations, pressing the pause button is crucial when dealing with lies. Our immediate response may be of hurt, but it is worth taking a step back to understand the reasons for your child telling a lie and to understand whether it is a once off or part of an ongoing pattern that you need to deal with.

Give your child a chance to tell the truth

Giving your child a chance to tell the truth, or warning them if you feel they are about to tell a lie, can help divert the problem and give a chance to own up:

> *Now before you answer, you know I will find out on Monday whether you really did any homework.*

> *I want you to think carefully before you answer.*

Simply and directly confront the lying

If your child tells a lie, the best response is to simply and directly confront this with the facts:

> *You were the only one in the room when the milk got spilt.*

> *I talked to your teacher and I know you didn't get a star.*

Have a consequence for the lie

Using a consequence can also be helpful in teaching your child to tell you the truth. If you do use a consequence, it is important that this is in addition to the consequence for the problem misbehaviour:

> *Because you spilt the milk, you are now going to have to clean it up. But also because you didn't tell the truth immediately, you are going to lose some TV time. It is really important that you learn to tell the truth.*

Prevention – Teaching Your Child To Tell The Truth

Talk about the importance of honesty

It can be useful to have a sit-down chat with your children about the importance of honesty and telling the truth. There are lots of good stories that you can read together with children about the importance and the value of trust (such as *The Little Boy who Cried Wolf*).

Remember, when talking to children about lying, asking them why they have told a lie is unlikely to help (you have to work that out yourself!). Generally, they won't know why and are likely to feel embarrassed or defensive. The best thing is to explain to them the importance of telling the truth and to help them learn how to communicate and deal with situations without telling lies (see Step 9).

Model honesty and trust

Children learn most by what parents do, rather than by what parents tell them to do. So if you model honesty to your child, this helps them to behave that way. This can mean owning up and apologising when you have made a mistake or let someone down, being straight and honest in how you talk to your children and your partner.

Reduce the opportunity for your child to tell lies

If your child has a tendency not to tell the whole truth in certain situations, make sure to structure things so they have little opportunity to do this. For example, if your child avoids homework, don't rely on them to report homework; make sure to check their homework diary with them. Some teachers operate a simple signature system whereby the teacher signs off the homework to be done and the parent signs that the child has tried to do it. This removes any opportunity for the child to understate what homework has to be done.

Encourage honesty

Always try to reward and encourage honesty. Simple comments like, 'I appreciate you being honest about what happened' or 'Thanks for telling me what happened' can make a difference. In addition, make sure to acknowledge honesty first when dealing with a discipline issue. For example, suppose your son comes to you and tells you that he has done something wrong; make sure to first acknowledge his honesty before dealing with the issue in hand: 'I appreciate you being honest and telling me … but you did something wrong and there needs to be a consequence.'

Address the underlying reason

In the long term it is best to take steps to address the reasons your child has gotten into a habit of lying. For example, if your son plays yourself and your partner off against one another ('Dad said I could go out'), then you can strive to make sure that you always communicate with your partner or that you always check things first with them.

Consider another example: if your daughter tells lies to gain approval ('I won a star in school') you could work hard to ensure your daughter gets approval and attention independent of these achievements or explore how she could gain the star legitimately:

> It sounds like you really want a star. Maybe if you do your homework well you might be able to get one; would you like me to help you?

> I know another way you can get star: I will make a star chart at home and each time you clean up the dishes I will give you a star. Would you like that?

You could also use the fact that your daughter has an elaborate imagination to her advantage. Make up stories with her about a little girl who goes on an adventure or succeeds in a special way and let her fill in the details. Such an activity might be a lovely way to spend time together and may prove a boost to her confidence. The long-term aim is to help your daughter learn and to gain your approval and attention and to feel happy about herself without resorting to lying.

Problem 12
Poor Bedtime Routine

Bedtime can be a nightmare with our four year old. She won't settle by herself and insists on story after story. When we leave her she often cries for us, saying she is thirsty or too warm. Sometimes she gets out of bed and comes down. It can take ages to finally get her settled, by which time we are all exhausted.

My ten year old is always battling to stay up late and to go to bed as late as me. It is really hard to get him to go to bed on time. Sometimes he stays up beyond ten and then he is exhausted in the morning and won't get up for school. It is very stressful.

Believe it or not, one of the most commons reasons for behaviour problems is tiredness caused by a poor bedtime routine. Aside from the conflict that happens when trying to get a reluctant child to bed, a late bedtime leaves the child very tired and more likely to be irritable in the morning, and even leads to underperformance in school. Further, a late bedtime for children usually means less time for parents alone to relax and recharge. This in turn leads to later bedtimes for parents, meaning that parents are also more likely to be stressed and tired, especially in the morning when it is important to have a relaxed, calm start to the day.

Children often need much more sleep than parents realise in order to function correctly the next day. Even children who seem to be high energy or on the go all the time (and thus appear not to need much sleep) often need a good night's sleep the most. Many of their problems can stem from over-tiredness and can be remedied (or at least made more manageable) when a good bedtime routine is established.

There are many different reasons as to why school-age children won't go to bed, but the two main ones are seeking to be in control and seeking parental attention. Many children find it hard to go to bed alone or feel that they are missing out if parents are still up without them. The long-term aim is to help children learn the skill of going to sleep alone and to ensure that they get a lot of good parental attention within a healthy and relaxing bedtime routine.

Prevention – Establishing A Good Bedtime Routine

Because routines are so central in positive parenting, a whole chapter is dedicated to them in this book (see Step 5). Probably the most important routine of all in ensuring happy children and parents is the bedtime routine. In addition to the principles in Step 5, below are some ideas for getting this established in your home.

Choose an early bedtime

The first step to changing a poor bedtime routine is to identify a clear and definite bedtime for your children. The most common mistake parents make is to set this too late for children. Given the need children have for sleep, generally it is best to aim for an earlier rather than a later bedtime (so even if there is some slippage, your children still get to bed at a reasonable time). It is perfectly fine to vary this time at weekends or on a rare special occasion (such as a visitor), when children are allowed to stay up a little later (with this then acting as a reward for children behaving well). It is ok to vary the bedtime depending on the age of your child. A good system can be for younger children to go to bed earlier than older ones. This also provides a good opportunity for one-to-one time with each of them as they prepare for bed.

Establish a relaxing routine before bed

Once a bedtime is established, the next step is to establish a relaxing routine leading up to bedtime that ideally allows plenty of time for getting ready and which schedules in some one-to-one parent–child time (such as reading or a night-time chat).

Sample routine for 8pm bedtime

7pm	Tidy away toys
7:10pm	Supper
7:30pm	Pyjamas on and in bedroom
7:40pm	Reading with Mum or Dad
8pm	Tuck in and good night

It is a good idea to leave children while they are still awake and to give them a chance to fall asleep by themselves. Some children continue to read for a few minutes after the parent has said goodnight and this can be built into the routine (fifteen minutes quiet time alone before lights out).

Check in on children

For young children it can be useful to agree to check in with them ten or fifteen minutes after bedtime (to tuck them in if they are still awake etc.). This works very well for children who are unsettled and who constantly call their parents after bedtime. In fact, you can make your checking-in dependent on them being quiet and not calling. For example, you can say to your child that you will only check in on them if they have been quiet for a few minutes first, and this will encourage them to settle.

Establish the routine on a chart

Doing up a chart with children that pictorially represents the routine steps, involving the children in making the chart and providing a reward each night when successfully completed are all things that can 'kick start' a bedtime routine and ensure it becomes a good habit (see Step 5 for a full explanation of these). You can decide the reward depending on which part of the routine your child finds difficult. For example, if your child gets to bed on time, but constantly leaves their bed at night, then you can give them 'one point' on the reward chart if they keep the routine prior to bedtime and 'double points' if they stay in bed all night.

Be patient

Establishing a bedtime routine can take a lot of time and patience, especially if your child has got into a habit of late bedtimes and if there has been ongoing battles about this. As discussed in Step 5, a useful approach is to gradually move towards an earlier bedtime.

For example, suppose your child has got into the habit of going to bed at 10pm when you go to bed – meaning that you don't get time alone and both you and your child are tired in the morning. Below are a number of steps to deal with this:

1. Decide on an ideal bedtime for your child – let's say 8:30pm.

2. Rather than switching immediately to 8:30pm – likely to be very hard – do this gradually.

3. Sit down with your child and explain that you are moving to an earlier bedtime of 8:30pm and you are going to do this gradually.

4. For the first night he has to be in bed by 9:55pm, the second night by 9:50pm and so on.

5. Give your child a small reward for each night he makes the target (e.g. a star or a point on a chart, which can be traded in for treats at the end of the week – see Step 5 for appropriate rewards).

In changing a child's behaviour it is often the first small step that is the most important – it doesn't matter how small it is as long as it is completed successfully. In the above example, if the child cooperates and goes to bed by himself, albeit only five minutes earlier, then a big step forward has been achieved.

Discipline – Responding When Children Won't Settle

Remain calm

As in all discipline situations, the key is to remain calm and not to provide too much attention to the child's misbehaviour (via lecturing, scolding, criticising etc.) and thus inadvertently reinforce the behaviour. Instead, the goal is to calmly and firmly insist on the rule.

If a young child leaves the bed or comes down, the best approach is to calmly take them back to bed, simply saying something like, 'Back to bed now please' and making sure they don't get any extra attention. When you first start to change a habit, this can take a lot of time and you may have to return a young child several times to bed. With older children you will need a back-up plan of consequences (see below).

Attend to children when they cooperate

A second key principle is to attend to children when they cooperate (even only to a small extent). For example, if a child is calling for attention from the bedroom, you can say:

When you are quiet for a minute, I will come and tuck you in.

When you lie back down in the bed, I will give you a kiss goodnight.

This can work with children leaving the bed in a similar way. You calmly take the child back to bed, giving only minimal attention and only attending to them and tucking them in when they are lying down in the bed. You can reinforce the discipline by emphasising the choice:

When you are back lying down quietly in your bed, I will come and tuck you in.

Use consequences and choices

Finally, establishing a system of consequences for bedtime is very helpful in ensuring children learn to cooperate. These are covered in detail in Step 7. A good consequence (that strikes most children as fair) is an earlier bedtime the following night.

For each minute you are out of bed tonight, you will have to go to bed a minute earlier tomorrow night.

As with all consequences, the key is to make them small and repeatable (one minute at a time) and to emphasise that the child has a choice – to behave and go to bed, or to experience the consequence.

It is also possible to use planned sanctions to help children cooperate. For example, if a child refuses to go to bed when asked or at the designated time, you can say:

Paul, if you don't start going to bed in the next minute, you are going to lose some pocket money.

Once again the key with consequences is to back off and give the child space to choose, as well as always remaining polite and firm (and even encouraging):

Come on Paul, I don't want you to lose any more money. Let's get these toys put away and you going to bed.

Problem 13
Stressed Parents

I find it so hard to do everything as a parent. I work long hours in a stressful job and then I come home to deal with stress with the kids. I am finding it hard to cope.

Sometimes I find myself being so resentful or negative towards the children. It makes me depressed to feel this way and I can feel so alone.

So many parents are extremely busy and pressured these days balancing work and family that they have little time for personal care and are out of touch with their own rising stress levels. Other parents become excessively focused on the problems and conflicts they have with their children, so they have little time to enjoy parenting, leading them to feel negative and depressed. In both these situations, not only is the parent liable to 'burn out' from stress and exhaustion, but their parenting becomes increasingly counter-productive, negative and resentful. Your own well-being as a parent is a significant factor in determining your child's well-being. Stressed or depressed parents find it hard to be positive and balanced in their parenting and many problems can become aggravated in these circumstances.

Caring For Parents

As we have said at the beginning of the book, parents should take time to look after their own needs as well as attending to the needs of their children. When parents' own needs for care, comfort and fulfilment are met, they are freed up to attend fully to the parenting role. Children need cared-for parents as much as they need parents to care for them. The best way to help your children grow up to be confident people with high self-esteem is for you as their parent to model this – that is, to take steps to value and prioritise yourself.

Seek support

If you feel stressed or depressed as a parent, the most important step you can take is to seek support from other people. When stressed or going through a hard time, the key is to realise that you are not alone; parents everywhere can appreciate what you are going through and most parents know what it is like to be struggling in the difficult job of being a parent. Support comes in many different forms such as:

- Setting time aside to talk with your partner
- Meeting a close friend
- Ringing a close family member
- Ringing a parenting helpline
- Accessing support from a parents' forum online
- Attending a parents' group
- Visiting a family resource centre
- Going to counselling.

The key is to make an active step to reach out to someone you trust and to seek support for what you are going through.

Create a balanced routine

Throughout the book we have talked about the importance of routines for children to help them learn good habits of behaving well. In the same way, routines that include time for parental relaxation and recreation are crucial to ensuring parents feel energised and cared for. Good routines are helpful for parents and children – for example, the benefits of an early bedtime for children are not only relaxed children but also relaxed parents (who gain important time to themselves in the evening). Essentially, creating a better routine can mean planning a more balanced work–life schedule that gives you more time with the family and more personal time, or making sure to plan a daily relaxation time as a parent, whether this is simply going for a walk or reading a book or ringing a close friend or watching a favourite TV programme. Find out what works for you as a parent. Consider the example below:

Joe worked in a very high-powered job that placed great demands on him. When he came home to his wife and children, he would frequently be preoccupied and stressed. Often he would be grumpy and snap angrily at his children over minor things. He used to collapse in front of the TV and not even have time to play with them. When he had time away, Joe began to reflect on how out of balance his life had become. He realised that his family and children were more important than his work and wanted to be there for them more. As a result, he began to change his working hours in an attempt to get home earlier. A useful routine he found was to take a fifteen minute walk through the park before he went home. During this time to himself, he would unwind and let the stress of the day go. He would prepare himself for arriving home, present and attentive to his children who would be demanding his attention.

Responding Constructively In The Moment

Press the pause button

A central principle throughout this book has been the importance of pausing in the immediacy of the moment. This gives you a chance to step back and to understand what is going on. It also gives you a chance to understand how you are feeling and thinking so you can see what the best course of action is. It gives you a chance to notice if you have been caught in negative thinking, or if you are over-reacting because you are stressed. Once you are self-aware, you can then choose your next step more constructively. This can be as simple as taking a moment to step back, taking a few deep breaths and acknowledging your feelings to yourself and your child – 'I'm sorry, I am just feeling a little bit stressed at the moment'.

Thinking constructively

Another way of remaining calm in difficult situations is to try to think positively about what is happening. When people react angrily or in an upset way, it is usually because they are thinking negatively about a situation.

Negative Thoughts Example

He is doing this on purpose ⟶ **Angry Reaction**
He is really a bold child

I am a hopeless parent ⟶ **Depressed Reaction**
I can't cope

The key is to become aware of your negative thoughts so they don't take over. The next step is to change how you are thinking about a situation and to have a more positive view, which in turn will lead you to have a more positive response and in time help your child behave more positively.

Positive Thoughts Example

He is testing me, but I will remain calm ⟶ **Positive Response**
The calmer I remain, the more I help him learn

My child has special needs, but the ⟶ **Positive Response**
calmer I remain, the more he learns

I am a good parent, doing my best ⟶ **Positive Response**
I am coping better each time

Affirmations

It is useful to practice thinking positive thoughts by writing them down as an affirmation so that you will remember them in a difficult situation. An example of a good affirmation is:

> *I am a calm, confident parent, doing my best for my child.*

Calmly repeating an affirmation to yourself can make your response more positive in the heat of the moment.

Special Issues

Issue 1

Helping Children Cope when Parents are Separated or Divorced

In recent times parental separation and divorce are much more common. More and more children are witnessing their parents separate and/or growing up in single parent households. The chain of events from parental conflict to separation and divorce can have a devastating impact on parents, children and extended families. In surveys, parental separation is second only to the death of a parent in the level of stress it can impart on children and parents. In addition, separation can lead to many other stressful events, such as house moves, money problems, legal battles, loss of supportive relationships, all of which can increase the burden on parents and children.

Helping Your Children Cope

The good news is that there are positive things you can do which will minimise the negative impact on your children. According to research studies, children can suffer a range of emotional and social difficulties on account of their parents' separation. However, a significant number of children cope relatively well and with the help of their parents can go on to lead happy lives post separation. How children cope *largely depends on how their parents manage the separation,* and parents can really help their children by proactively taking steps to deal with the separation in as positive a manner as possible. There are a number of practical things that you can do:

1. Take steps to manage your own stress to ensure you are personally coping.
2. Work constructively with your former partner on parenting issues.
3. Help your children cope with divided loyalty.
4. Listen to your children and focus on their best interests and needs.
5. Minimise the moves and changes in your child's life post separation.

1. Take steps to manage your own stress to ensure you are personally coping

Separation is often a very stressful time for parents and it is normal to experience a rollercoaster of emotions, from upset and rage to anger and shame. Many parents understandably become preoccupied with their own concerns before and after a separation and some parents can become stuck in resentment or bitterness or feeling depressed at what they have lost. Your children do need you at this time, but the first step to healing is to start to care for yourself. Take whatever steps are necessary to get the support you need to cope, whether this is by going to counselling or a support group or confiding in a close friend. As you begin to cope you will be more available to your children.

2. Work constructively with your former partner on parenting issues

One of the biggest things that damage children in a family is witnessing or suffering the effects of ongoing conflict between parents. In fact, the level of hostility and conflict between parents is a real predictor of stress and problems for children, *whether the parents live together or not*. (Indeed, some children actually do better after parental separation if the new arrangement leads to less conflict and a more harmonious family environment.) For this reason, it is crucial that you work hard to develop a constructive relationship with your ex-partner. Though this can be hard work (especially if you have old hurts), it is the single biggest factor that will help your children cope. The more you can agree living and contact arrangements amicably and focus on your children's interests, the better your children will cope. A good way to do this is to develop a 'business-like' relationship with your ex-partner – your aim is to move on from the past and to work constructively together as co-parents. If this proves difficult, do consider going to mediation services.

3. Help your children cope with divided loyalty

It is very common for children to experience a *divided sense of loyalty between their parents*. Be wary of inadvertently involving the children in the parental dispute. In particular:

- Make sure to give your children a balanced and fair account of the separation and what happened that is appropriate to their age and understanding. Reassure them that both their parents still love them. Ideally, this message should be given by both parents together or separately and repeated many times.

- Speak positively about your ex-partner in front of the children, or, if you can't, be honest that these are *your* feelings and that your child has a right to feel differently. Even if your child appears not to care or is negative about their other parent, remember that this could just be because they are hiding their emotions and feel they have to be loyal to you.

- Don't use your child as a 'go between' i.e. don't communicate to your ex-partner through your kids. If you need to discuss something with your ex, arrange a time to do this face to face or on the phone, and don't ask your children to pass on a message.

4. Listen to your children and focus on their best interests and needs

Children cope differently with their parents' separation depending on their age and personality. Listen carefully to your children individually to understand what support they need. Even children who appear to be coping well need special understanding. It is a good idea to make sure that you have one-to-one time with your kids where they have an opportunity to open up and talk. Periodically raise the topic of the separation and ask them how they are coping. As they get older they will have further questions and thoughts. The ideal situation is when they can talk to you about their feelings and ask questions as they need to. Work hard at keeping the lines of communication open.

5. Minimise the moves and changes in your child's life post separation

Sometimes the major losses in children's lives are not directly due to the separation itself. Often they are related to the other changes that the children experience (e.g. moving house, leaving a school, losing friends because of a move, not seeing grandparents as often). While parents often feel they need a 'fresh start' (e.g. a move to a new location) post separation, research seems to suggest that children need the opposite. Try to maintain as many of the good things in your child's life post separation as possible. For example, this might mean making a special effort to ensure they keep in contact with grandparents or relatives from the other side of the family, or ensuring they can stay in the same school and see the same friends. These continuities do much to help a child cope.

Finally, remember that even though separation can be a traumatic event for the family, you can take action and help you and your children cope.

Further reading

John Sharry, Peter Reid, Eugene Donohoe, *When Parents Separate: Helping your Children Cope*, Dublin, Veritas, 2001.

Issue 2
Encouraging Safety on the Internet

As a parent, the internet can be great source of worry and concern. We hear in the media all the stories of internet abuses, from cyber bullying to children accessing unsuitable material such as pornography or, worse still, being subjected to grooming by paedophiles. Even aside from the headline scares above, parents have other concerns about using computers, such as worrying about whether their children's computer usage is excessive and interfering with school work or more healthy leisure pursuits.

In trying to decide the best way to monitor computer usage, parents can feel at a loss, especially if they are not technically savvy themselves or if their adolescent children know more about the internet and computers than they do. Below are a number of principles for dealing with these issues with children and teenagers.

There Are Good Aspects To Using Computers

The first thing to remember is that using computers and the internet is not all bad for children. In fact, there is a lot of learning and entertainment and even social benefits to using computers for children. Children can use the internet as an aid to doing homework and as a resource for school projects. Furthermore, given the fact the computers are so integrated into society and work, it is important that children learn how to use them and become familiar with them as they grow up. So, rather than imposing an outright ban, your job as a parent is to support them in learning to use computers responsibly and healthily.

At What Age Should Children Start Using A Computer?

There is no lower age limit for children's use of a computer. In fact, there are many pieces of educational software and quality websites (such as the BBC) targeted at preschool children, which have fun and educational benefits for young children. Once usage is well supervised and part of a balanced routine, then children can start learning to use computers at any age.

At What Age Should Children Use Email?

A more important age threshold is when children are allowed to communicate to other children on the internet (via email or the social networking sites). Children should only be allowed to have an email when they have a reason for one (e.g. a friend or family member to communicate with) and are mature enough to use one responsibly. In many ways, it is a similar decision to when a child can have a mobile phone. This is a personal judgement for families, but I would recommend no younger than twelve years old. Most social networking sites such as BEBO have an age limit of thirteen years old.

Before allowing a child to use email or social networking sites, make sure that they are responsible enough to do so. Just as you would with a mobile phone, sit down with them and explain the dangers (inappropriate emails etc.) and make sure that they know to come to you if anything worries them. Say to them also that you will be supervising their email usage. With young pre-teen children it is acceptable and appropriate to read and check every email they send or receive.

You Are In Charge As A Parent

The second point to remember is that, as the parent, you are in charge of the computer use in your home. Children and adolescents should not be given free reign or access and you should take control and establish rules about computer and internet usage.

Install safety software

Install safety software such as NetNanny on the computer which allows you to restrict and monitor your children's usage. Each child is given a password that allows them to access the internet (which you control). The best way to start with children is to set up the software so that *you have to approve in advance each website they want to access.*

Public place

Make sure that the computer with internet access is in a public place and not in their bedroom.

Establish rules about your child's usage

Rather than allowing unlimited access, make sure computer usage is part of a balanced routine (e.g. half an hour a day on a school night and an hour at the weekends) or alternatively only when homework is done and not immediately before bedtime – when a more relaxing activity such as reading may be a better choice.

Monitor your child's usage

Depending on your child's age, it is appropriate to check what your child is accessing on the internet or what emails they are sending or receiving. Children and young teenagers are very vulnerable and need protecting. It is a good idea to explain to them in advance that you will be doing this.

Encouraging Responsible Usage

As children become older, the goal is to help them use the internet responsibly and to help them learn how to protect themselves from danger.

- Sit down regularly with your children and talk to them about their internet usage. Ask them to show you what they access on the net and to tell you what appeals to them about using it. Take an interest in what they are doing.

- Talk about the dangers of the internet. Get their views and ask what they would do should they come across unsuitable material or be approached by a stranger or was bullied online. Encourage them to come and talk to you if anything worries them.

The Dangers Of The Internet

As a parent you should be aware of the dangers and the problems that can arise in internet usage, such as:

- Cyber-bullying – whereby your child is subject to bullying by email or comments made on social networking sites or in chat rooms
- Viewing inappropriate material on the internet (such as pornography or hate sites)
- Making contact with unsuitable people in chat rooms
- Excessive or 'addictive' internet usage that is interfering with school work or other healthy pursuits.

Spotting the danger signs

You may get warnings that your child is in trouble on the internet, such as:

- Being excessively secret or hiding their activity on the internet
- Spending an excessive amount of time on the internet
- Changes in mood or behaviour
- Appearing depressed or worried, especially after being on the internet.

What to do when you are concerned

The first step is to talk to your child about your concerns. Pick a good time to start a conversation and be very specific about your concerns:

You seem to be quite upset after using the internet; is there anything wrong?

I notice you have been viewing this site on the net, and I don't think that it is suitable.

I feel you are using the internet too much these days; we need to establish some rules about doing homework.

The next step then is to listen to their account of what is going on so you can get a sense of whether the situation is serious or not, and then agree a plan of action. Remember that children can easily come across unsuitable material by accident or as a 'once off' out of curiosity, so it is important to listen and discuss the issues rather than jumping to conclusions. If it is a serious situation, do seek support from the appropriate professional services such as school staff, the police etc.

For more information on safe and educational internet usage and for tips on protecting children and young people, consult the Internet Advisory Board on www.iab.ie.

Seeking Further Help

This book has been written as a 'self-help' resource for parents. My aim has been to provide you with information that can empower you in the valuable and important job of bringing up children. This is not to say that parents don't need lots of support.

Parenting works best when you have lots of on-going support from other people (such as extended family and friends) and access to special support and services when faced with special difficulties. For this reason, it is important that you do seek further help as and when you need it.

An important source of support is often from your child's teacher or childminder. Many common children's problems (as do many of the solutions) occur in school. It is important that you work in partnership with your children's teachers. A lot of research studies have shown that children do best when their parents are closely involved in their education and have good working relationships with their teachers. In addition, by working with the school you can often gain extra supports for your child; for example, educational psychology, remedial help, after-school services. The school is often the first port of call in gaining extra help for your child.

In addition, you can seek help from other professional services such as the health visitor or baby nurse when your child is young, or your family GP. Most areas have a child and family centre or a family resource centre or a variety of playgroups and parents groups which can provide lots of helpful services to you and your children. Do check out what resources are available in your local area.

Finally, you might find it useful to do a parenting course or take part in a parenting group. Many parents find it immeasurably helpful to meet other parents in similar situations, gaining support and new ideas. Parenting groups are very common and are often run from your local family resource centre or school or even the local adult education centre. The addresses and websites that follow can be used as a starting point in your search for information about the services that best suit you.

The essential thing is to make sure you get out there and get the help you need. Good luck!

Websites and Resources

Below are a list of websites and resources that can be helpful in seeking extra support and information wherever you are currently living. The list is by no means exhaustive but rather a starting point of useful websites.

Barnardos www.barnardos.com
Leading children's charity with information and supports for parents. Links to national Barnardos websites in Ireland, UK, Australia and New Zealand.

Family Support Agency www.fsa.ie
Details of family resource centres and supports throughout Ireland.

Parentline www.parentline.ie
Irish website providing support for parents.

Parentline Plus www.parentlineplus.org.uk
National UK charity that works for, and with, parents; website with a range of useful parenting information and excellent links.

Parentline Australia www.parentline.com.au
Support website based in Australia.

www.parenting.org
A well-organised parenting website set up by a non-profit child care organisation in America.

www.kidshealth.org
High quality and popular American family health website with information for parents, teens and children.

www.babycentre.co.uk
High quality baby health and parenting information. Links to equivalent national websites throughout the world.

www.vhi.ie
Irish health website, with forums and expert advice on health and family issues.

www.rollercoaster.ie
An excellent Irish-based parenting resource, full of useful articles, bulletin boards and links. Also sends out regular newsletters to subscribers.

Further Reading (by the author)

Parenting books

Sharry, J., Hampson, G. & Fanning, M., *Parenting Preschoolers and Young Children: A Practical Guide to Promoting Confidence Learning and Good Behaviour*, Dublin, Veritas, 2005.

Fitzpatrick, C. & Sharry, J., *Coping with Depression in Young People – A Guide for Parents*, Chichester, Wiley, 2004.

Sharry, J., *Parent Power: Bringing up Responsible Children and Teenagers*, Chichester, Wiley, 2002.

Sharry, J., *Bringing up Responsible Teenagers*, Dublin, Veritas, 2001.

Sharry, J., Reid, P. & Donohoe, E., *When Parents Separate: A Guide to Helping You and your Children Cope*, Dublin, Veritas, 2001.

Counselling Books

Sharry, J., *Solution Focused Groupwork* (2nd ed.), London, Sage, 2007.

Sharry, J., *Counselling Children, Adolescents and Families: A Strengths-Based Collaborative Approach*, London, Sage, 2004.

Sharry, J., Madden, B. & Darmody, M., *Becoming a Solution-Focused Detective: Identifying your Client Strengths in Brief Therapy*, NY, Haworth, 2003.

Parenting programmes for group leaders

Parents Plus Early Years Programme: A dvd-based parenting course to promoting young children's development and to preventing and managing behaviour problems aged 1 to 6.

Parents Plus Children's Progamme: A dvd-based parenting course to managing behaviour problems and promoting learning in children aged 6 to 11.

Parents Plus Adolescents Progamme: A dvd-based course to managing conflict and getting on better with older children and teenagers aged 11 to 16.

Further Details

Parents Plus Charity c/o Mater Hospital, North Circular Road, Dublin 7. www.parentsplus.ie.